...as Keller ■ Fleur De Lys • Hubert Keller ■ Masa's • Ron Siegel ■ Antonello • Fra...
• Laurent Méchin ■ BlackBird • Paul Kahan ■ Nomi • Sandro Gamba ■ The Fren...
...stein ■ Caffe Abbracci • Nino Pernetti ■ Mark's Las Olas • Ma... ...tia...
...a • Lidia Bastianich & Fortunato Nicotra ■ La Caravelle • Troy Du... ...Dav...
...sco" Ricchi ■ Gerard's Place • Gerard Pangaud ■ Melrose • Brian McBride ■ Aria
• Anthony Musarra ■ Rockpool • Neil Perry ■ Tetsuya • Tetsuya Akuda ■ Grissini
...Harbour Road • Li Shu -Tim ■ Sabatini • Francesco Brocca ■ Au Jardin des Amis • Ch...
...goire Simonin ■ Shang Palace • Peter Tsang ■ Shiraishi • Shinji Shiraishi ■ Enote...
...Joel Robuchon • Yosuke Suga ■ Monna Lisa • Toru Kawano ■ New York Grill • Br...
• David Rood ■ Le Gavroche • Michel Roux ■ Langan's Brasserie • Richard Shepherd
...osimann ■ Turner's • Brian Turner ■ Bistrot du Sommelier • Jean-André Lalican ■
...rat ■ Bistro Jeanty • Phillipe Jeanty ■ Bouchon/The French Laundry • Jeffery Cerciello
...Franco Barone • Crustacean • Helene An ■ La Cachette • Jean Francois Meteigner ■
...ench Room • William Koval ■ Mansion at Turtle Creek • Dean Fearing ■ Azul • Miche...
...an's • Michel Focqeteau ■ Herbsaint • Donald Link ■ Rene's Bistrot • Rene Bajeux
...David Feau ■ San Domenico • Odette Fada ■ Citronelle • Michel Richard ■ Etrusco
...Matthew Moran ■ Est • Peter Doyle ■ Galileo • Harunobu Inukai ■ Harbour Kitch...
...ittorio Lucariello ■ Inagiku • Yumoto Makoto ■ Margaux • Christopher Christie ■ O...
...f Galvin Lim ■ Les Amis • Justin Quek ■ Raffles • David Mollicome, Jean-Paul Naqui...
...a Pinchiorri • Chef Toshikazu Tsugi & Chef Olivier ■ Kozue • Kenichiro Ooe ■ L'Atelier
...tterson & Matthew Crabbe ■ Bombay Brasserie • Adi Modi & Vikram Sunderam ■ Hush
...n's team ■ Le Manoir aux Quat' Saisons • Raymond Blanc ■ Mosimann • Anton Mosima...
...Yannick Alenoo ■ Le Park • Christophe David ■ La Ribaudiere • Thierry Verrat ■ Bis...
■ Fleur De Lys • Hubert Keller ■ Masa's • Ron Siegel ■ Antonello • Franco Baro...
...nt Méchin ■ BlackBird • Paul Kahan ■ Nomi • Sandro Gamba ■ The French Room
...Caffe Abbracci • Nino Pernetti ■ Mark's Las Olas • Mark Militello ■ Christian's • Mic...
...a Bastianich & Fortunato Nicotra ■ La Caravelle • Troy Dupuy ■ Lutéce • David Feau
...Gerard's Place • Gerard Pangaud ■ Melrose • Brian McBride ■ Aria • Matthew Mor...
...a ■ Rockpool • Neil Perry ■ Tetsuya • Tetsuya Akuda ■ Grissini • Vittorio Lucarie...
...Li Shu -Tim ■ Sabatini • Francesco Brocca ■ Au Jardin des Amis • Chef Galvin Lim
...l Shang Palace • Peter Tsang ■ Shiraishi • Shinji Shiraishi ■ Enoteca Pinchiorri • C...
...osuke Suga ■ Monna Lisa • Toru Kawano ■ New York Grill • Brett Patterson & Matth...
...Gavroche • Michel Roux ■ Langan's Brasserie • Richard Shepherd & Langan's team ■
• Brian Turner ■ Bistrot du Sommelier • Jean-André Lalican ■ Le Meurice • Yann...
...Phillipe Jeanty ■ Bouchon/The French Laundry • Jeffery Cerciello & Thomas Keller ■ Fl...
...ean • Helene An ■ La Cachette • Jean Francois Meteigner ■ Pavilion • Laurent Méc...
■ Mansion at Turtle Creek • Dean Fearing ■ Azul • Michelle Bernstein ■ Caffe Abbra...
...Herbsaint • Donald Link ■ Rene's Bistrot • Rene Bajeux ■ Felidia • Lidia Bastianich...
...) • Odette Fada ■ Citronelle • Michel Richard ■ Etrusco • "Cesco" Ricchi ■ Gerar...
• Peter Doyle ■ Galileo • Harunobu Inukai ■ Harbour Kitchen • Anthony Musarra...
...giku • Yumoto Makoto ■ Margaux • Christopher Christie ■ One Harbour Road • Li S...
• Justin Quek ■ Raffles • David Mollicome, Jean-Paul Naquin & Gregoire Simonin ■ Sha...
...zu Tsugi & Chef Olivier ■ Kozue • Kenichiro Ooe ■ L'Atelier de Joel Robuchon • Yosu...
■ Bombay Brasserie • Adi Modi & Vikram Sunderam ■ Hush • David Rood ■ Le Gavro...
...Quat' Saisons • Raymond Blanc ■ Mosimann • Anton Mosimann ■ Turner's • Br...
...e Park • Christophe David ■ La Ribaudiere • Thierry Verrat ■ Bistro Jeanty • Phill...
• Hubert Keller ■ Masa's • Ron Siegel ■ Antonello • Franco Barone ■ Crustacean
...ckBird • Paul Kahan ■ Nomi • Sandro Gamba ■ The French Room • William Koval
• Nino Pernetti ■ Mark's Las Olas • Mark Militello ■ Christian's • Michel Focqeteau
...ortunato Nicotra ■ La Caravelle • Troy Dupuy ■ Lutéce • David Feau ■ San Domen...
...ce • Gerard Pangaud ■ Melrose • Brian McBride ■ Aria • Matthew Moran ■ Est
...pool • Neil Perry ■ Tetsuya • Tetsuya Akuda ■ Grissini • Vittorio Lucariello ■ Inag...
■ Sabatini • Francesco Brocca ■ Au Jardin des Amis • Chef Galvin Lim ■ Les Amis
...lace • Peter Tsang ■ Shiraishi • Shinji Shiraishi ■ Enoteca Pinchiorri • Chef Toshika...
...l ■ Monna Lisa • Toru Kawano ■ New York Grill • Brett Patterson & Matthew Crabbe
• Michel Roux ■ Langan's Brasserie • Richard Shepherd & Langan's team ■ Le Manoir a...
...ner ■ Bistrot du Sommelier • Jean-André Lalican ■ Le Meurice • Yannick Alenoo
...anty • Bouchon/The French Laundry • Jeffery Cerciello & Thomas Keller ■ Fleur De Lys
...ne An ■ La Cachette • Jean Francois Meteigner ■ Pavilion • Laurent Méchin ■ BlackB...
...n at Turtle Creek • Dean Fearing ■ Azul • Michelle Bernstein ■ Caffe Abbracci • N...
...t • Donald Link ■ Rene's Bistrot • Rene Bajeux ■ Felidia • Lidia Bastianich & Fortun...
...tte Fada ■ Citronelle • Michel Richard ■ Etrusco • "Cesco" Ricchi ■ Gerard's Place

Found in a Buddhist Temple in Tokyo

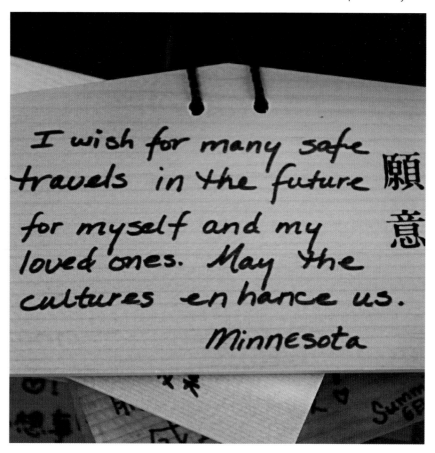

Dedicated to my Mum & Dad, Sheila Joy & Laurie, who gave life to my epicurean odyssey, the innocence of my son Adam, and the inspiration of my beloved Nadia that has brought forth this harvest of wonderful places, people, and pabulum!

Bon ViVant Publishing Inc
1601 West MacArthur Boulevard Suite 6G
South Coast Metro Ca 92704 USA

Design & Production by Nathan Stein, Digital Imagery & Design
Photography by Jeff Markowitz, directed by David Shaw
Recipes excerpted from The Bouchon Cookbook © 2004 by Thomas Keller
Used by permission of Artisan, a division of Workman Publishing Co., Inc.

Printed In Belgium
0-9722750-1-0
Library of Congress cataloguing - in - Publication Data
Bon ViVant Publishing, Inc.

The Art of Excellence –
Chefs, Cuisine, Cities, & Cognacs

David Shaw, International First Impressions,
Bon ViVant Publishing Inc. and CLS Rémy-Cointreau

ISBN 0-9722750-1-0

THE ART OF EXCELLENCE

Chefs, Cuisine, Cities, & Cognacs

INTRODUCTION

Hello Dear Reader,

My name is Roger Moore.

Before I formally introduce you to the pleasurable dining that is to be had from this epically unique Guidebook, let me take a moment of your time to talk to you about my work with UNICEF and what it means to me. ▪ I first became involved with UNICEF by a virtual epiphany...I was escorting Audrey Hepburn, the then - international spokeswoman for UNICEF at an event in 1990 (a TV show- the Danny Kay Children's Awards Show in Amsterdam) Kay was the original goodwill ambassador for UNICEF in 1946. At an earlier press conference before the show, Audrey spoke...and she spoke...and spoke...But only about UNICEF not about her international stardom...she spoke with such passion and emotion and clarity of thought...I was overwhelmed and the following year, when I was invited back, I had become consumed with just having to know more about this most humane and noble cause. Then, 40,000 children were dying a day...today this has been reduced to 28,000, but that is still 28,000 too many! My first trip was in 1992 to El Salvador...I have been traveling the world as a volunteer ever since...and as long as I live, I will always be involved. Paid members have to retire at 60, but volunteers such as myself, Harry Belafonte, Pierce Brosnan and Peter Ustinov renew our membership every year and continue until we literally drop! My calendar usually means that for nine months of the year I am engaged in the field with UNICEF projects and visits. Although I can request a location the practice is to send you wherever you are needed. Inevitably these days I get a lot of requests and invitations over and above the UNICEF program and I find it difficult to refuse because if it means that you have the chance to spread the word further about UNICEF, then you just have to accept it and do it! ▪ UNICEF (United Nations International Children's Emergency Fund) is a world organization with minimum overheads - for every dollar received, only nine cents is retained for administration...the rest goes into the field. There are thirty - seven countries involved in raising money to help children suffering from war, disease, famine, malnutrition. Money in the main is raised by lobbying the governments of the world through UNICEF's 37 committees. ▪ In any of the restaurants featured in this book, you will be able to purchase your own copy at a favorable price. From the ensuing sales of this, all the proceeds will be donated to the United Nations International Children's Emergency Fund (UNICEF). To this end, and on behalf of UNICEF, I would like to thank David Shaw (Author), Rémy Martin, and especially the restaurants for their commitment and dedication to UNICEF's cause. ▪ That said, I am now genuinely delighted to formally introduce to you, The Art of Excellence, which typifies a journey of taste and expectancy...a journey where you will enjoy the many shapes, flavors and aromas of a myriad cities and its cuisines...and all from the comfort of your armchair. ▪ Throughout this journey, David Shaw, the author of the earlier sister volume Spirit of Excellence and publisher of the magazine First Impressions of International Dining and Bon ViVant, will guide you through this magnificent demonstration of quite inspired and ingenious signature dishes from several celebrated restaurants around the universe. ▪ I am also further pleased to inform you will also be able to attempt cooking many of these fabulous dishes by playing the attached CD-ROM, which contains the fully illustrated recipes of these famous signature dishes. ▪ Again, thank you for your "Excellent" support of UNICEF in buying this book, I hope you enjoy it as much as I have...and don't forget to tell your family and friends!

Sir Roger Moore, KBE

International Goodwill Ambassador for UNICEF
November 2003.

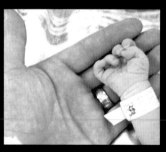

...there is no finer investment for any community than putting milk into babies... ...or...for the eliminated...

...as an International Goodwill Ambassador for UNICEF (there are others such as Harry Belafonte and Peter Ustinov) Sir Roger Moore KBE, for over a decade now, spends nine months of the year traveling around the universe to the worst scenes of carnage suffering and famine. With his beloved and devoted wife Kristina beside him, he has raised, through his tireless unstinting physical presence and efforts, millions of dollars for the benefit of UNICEF (the United Nations International Children's Emergency Fund). ▪ *So what has all this got to with this book?* ▪ Well, let's describe my feelings about why I always wanted to produce such a book...I am obsessed with the pursuit of all things excellent...namely wines and food...It is a science ...it truly is an art...These restaurants are art...the chefs are artists...their food - works of art on a plate, their canvas... ▪ In Cognac, Rémy Martin is steeped in the art of taking the fine champagne cognac grapes that are indigenous to the region...the making of their prestigious and most respected product is indeed an art of excellence... the cities chosen in this book represent true excellence...this book is about the art of their collective excellence... and, of course and above all, TASTE. ▪ Many readers will have in my first volume – The Spirit of Excellence, encountered for the first time, the pairing of great signature dishes with the collection of Rémy Martin Fine Champagne Cognacs...It was both a revelation and an education of the palate as much as the advancement of that taste... ▪ That book helped me to strengthen and further the strong bond, I have always enjoyed through my publications First Impressions International and more recently Bon Vivant, with so many of the USA's Master Chefs. Subsequently because of their involvement and the formidable presence and voice of Rémy -Martin (France) and Rémy Amerique (USA) I was able to approach many of the brilliant chefs outside the USA... ▪ Through these activities, I was also able to meet and propose to Roger Moore (he wasn't a knight then!) that through the support of these great culinary luminaries and through Rémy Martin's sponsorship, further substantial amounts could be raised to help the plight of children the world over. And of course, inevitably through Roger's colossal presence, we could embark on not only further fine publications of this nature in support of this most humanitarian of causes, but also a series of charity "Rémy –only" banquets, where perhaps Roger (UNICEF calendar permitting –at time of press he is in Cambodia!) and some of his fellow celebrities and UNICEF associates could attend and speak...

'If you can dream, and not make dreams your master;
'f you can think, and not make thoughts your aim;
'f you can meet with Triumph and Disaster and treat those two impostors just the same...
Yours is the Earth and everything that's in it, And, which is more, you'll be a Man, my son!"
  "If " by Rudyard Kipling...

In his heroic quest, he is one of UNICEF's most effective and sought - after goodwill ambassadors, raising for the cause, millions of dollars. With his devoted and equally committed wife Kristina, by his side throughout, he has walked that extra 1000 miles in the company of kings, and queens, presidents and prime ministers and even just the common man – all simply for...the children. By buying this book you will be making a considerable donation to UNICEF... Thank you for your humanity. ▪ So here we are at the embarkation of this magnificent Epicurean voyage...I hope you are happy and sated with all the scents, shapes, textures of a myriad countries' spices and flavors in your own pursuit of the Art of Excellence.

▪ As you read and enjoy the photographic imagery of the excellence of life in the many cities, you will be able to embrace the wonderful cuisine of these same locations, through the creative eyes of many of their world's leading chefs. You will be able to enjoy a myriad cuisines at their stellar best, either at the restaurants in person, or by entertaining friends and family at home by emulating the same dishes, as detailed in the Recipe CD-ROM, which you will find, attached at the beginning of this book. At the same time you will discover through the fine champagne cognac that is quintessentially Rémy Martin, "the art of excellently" pairing these fine cognacs with the exquisite dishes of the world's greatest restaurants.

Taste, Understand, Enjoy

David Shaw

(Author of Spirit of Excellence and Publisher of
Bon Vivant -Crème de la Crème Dining)

TABLE
OF
CONTENTS

FOR RECIPES OF SIGNATURE
DISHES, SEE CD-ROM

PREFACE

by Vincent Géré

Maître Dégustateur
de Rémy Martin

" I love this book because it is a celebration of food and cognac which fires the imagination. As it explores and explains, it is a perfect introduction to great cognacs for the beginner. The cognac connoisseur can also learn from it. This is a new book exploring a very old subject, a modern taste of an ancient spirit. Here are the ultimate tastings in dishes and pairings where you can smell, enjoy and learn at the same time. The aim is to take you inside the glass, to immerse you in the atmosphere of the restaurants and our cellars: to make the cognac live for you. We feel that understanding cognac selection will help you enjoy it more. What I call becoming 'cognac intelligent'."

For as long as I can remember, I have always enjoyed the best bottles at the table. I have a clear memory of my childhood, growing up between Cognac and Bordeaux, with my father, a winemaker and cognac maker, asking me what I thought of this or that rare sample from a winery, distillery or other cellar. Generally these tastings took place over dessert or cheese at the end of a Sunday lunch. ■ Naturally, when I became a winemaker myself, I continued to match wines, champagnes and cognacs from the Fine Champagne area with food. I remember challenging sessions with Daniel Thibault, the Chef de Cave of Charles Heidsieck Champagne, seeking to find a precise match for his latest 'babies' with selected bouchées, tasting-sized portions of a variety of dishes. ■ During my years as Winemaker at the Blue Pyrenees Estate in Australia, it even got to the point where I was working on my blends of Australian wines during lunch, seeing how they reacted and getting to know them better. Over thirty trips to China setting up wineries there for Rémy Martin, I discovered the culture of celebrating with cognacs throughout banquets where there were up to fifteen dishes and their complex spices with which to play. ■ As I became more and more involved in the making of Rémy Martin cognacs, it quickly became obvious to me how lucky I was to be experiencing the ultimate concentration of wine flavors. The eaux-de-vie are from the best vineyards, the distillation on the lees concentrates their textures, and the richness from the long ageing in barrels corresponds to a maturation level rarely seen in wines. ■ I entered the territory of perfume you can drink: Top notes, aromatic heart, base notes, first sip, mouth-feel, balance of the finish, length – twenty, fifty, a hundred flavors at a time; two hundred, three hundred, seven hundred cognacs present in one assemblage, ten times the complexity of great wines. Working on the blends is a challenge for your taste, for all your points of reference. Here in Cognac, we are bathed in French culture and memories. A very different cultural experience compared to a tasting during a Chinese banquet in Shanghai! ■ We started working on matching food and cognacs with French chefs, in the Cognac region at first. The 'Only Rémy' Dinners were born. The restaurant kitchens became real taste laboratories as the chefs discovered the varied possibilities in pairing food with our cognacs. Their understanding changed, as did ours, it was almost as if they were re-inventing our cognacs for us, helping to understand the criterias of quality which are important to them and their clients. ■ When I met David Shaw, I discovered someone with the same natural belief in food and tasting as important cultural experiences. He saw the differences this way of looking at things can create. From this point, we embarked on the biggest of adventures, travelling throughout the great cities of the United States and then of the world. Our goal was simple, if ambitious: to work with the greatest chefs, all important personalities of achievements, passion and with a genuine need to experiment with flavors. In other words, to unleash *TASTE*. ■ So the adventure consists of pairing our cognacs with the best signature dishes from some of the best chefs in the world. This selective focus reveals spectacular facets of our cognacs because each dish brings out different and unique aspects. Further on in the book, I have explained the fundamentals of tasting and pairing, how to look for matches, synergies, fusions. Give each pairing the luxury of time: it is a price worth paying to savor rare aromas, huge flavors, delicate textures on the palate, balanced finish, layers of finesse, incredible length. ■ I trust that apart from enjoying the food served at the restaurants featured in this book, the recipes will make you want to rush down to your local deli or wine merchant before cooking and opening one or more of the Fine Champagne cognacs in the Rémy Martin range. V.S.O.P; 1738 Accord Royal; X.O Excellence; Extra; Louis XIII : now you can TASTE them, fired with enthusiasm and confidence... the choice is yours! ■ Thank you to these great Chefs for allowing all of us at Rémy Martin to fall in love all over again with our very special cognacs.

Vincent Géré
Maître Dégustateur de Rémy Martin

THE
ART OF
EXCELLENT
COGNAC

COGNAC

COGNAC the place is a town of quiet charm in western France, north of Bordeaux. Its medieval heart lies on the Charente River (*'the prettiest stream in all my kingdom'*, said Henri IV four hundred years ago) which winds its placid way through the area entitled to make the spirit that is Cognac. The landscape is gentle and clothed with over a quarter of a million acres of vineyards.

All cognacs are brandies but not all brandies are cognacs...

There have been vines on this land since Roman times, but Cognac, as we know it, dates from the last half of the seventeenth century when, for reasons not entirely certain but probably to do with taxes and economics of transport, the Cognaçais switched from shipping their wine to distilling it into the spirit first called brandewijn by the Dutch and *'burnt wine'* by the English, its two main export markets. So brandy was born: the only spirit – as it still is today – to be distilled from grapes rather than grain. ■ At first, brandy was most popular with the military for its medicinal properties. Both the British and Dutch navies used it to 'sterilize' the impure water their ships carried at sea while both navies and armies recognized its antiseptic qualities on wounds and 'anaesthetic' abilities (when drunk in large quantities) if musket balls had to be removed or limbs amputated. It is probably safe to say that this brandy had neither the taste nor complexity of cognac today. ■ By the nineteenth century the Cognac area was the largest grape-growing region in the world although its wines were almost all distilled. As quality improved and brandies started to be named according to the region they came from, they were further defined by area and quality. Champagne de Cognac (referring to the region just below Cognac the town) was considered superior to brandy from the Bois (the wooded areas nearer the coast) and so commanded a higher price. This is still true today. ■ Given the French obsession with the quality of their food and wine, it was only to be expected that quality controls would eventually apply to Cognac. In 1909 a decree of the French government specified the geographic area of Cognac and marked it out into six regions, or crus. ■ From the twin centers, named Grande Champagne and Petite Champagne (the word champagne in French originally meant *"open countryside"* and here has nothing to do with bubbles), the other four – Borderies, Fins Bois, Bons Bois and Bois Ordinaires – spread out in roughly concentric rings towards the Atlantic coast. Only brandies made within these borders could legally be called cognac, a decree reinforced in 1938, when each of the crus was awarded its own Appellation d'Origine Contrôlée (AOC). From then on also, only cognac made from Grande Champagne and Petite Champagne grapes (with at least half from the former) could be called Fine Champagne Cognac. The word *'fine'* on its own on a cognac bottle is virtually meaningless.

"Everyone knows two words of French and one of them is Cognac- A place of Spirit and the Spirit of a place. Both are special."

The essence of wine, country and lifestyle

The Rémy Martin Dynasty...

At the end of the seventeenth century, as brandy was entering adolescence, a young boy was tending the vines on his family's farm at Rouillac, about 15 miles from Cognac. His name was Rémy, the son of Denis and Marie Martin. He grew into an ambitious and clever young man who could see the future in distilling. He added more vineyards to the family property and by 1724, married and prosperous, he was ready to expand. The House of Rémy Martin, growers and merchants, was formed. ■ He was to be the only Cognaçais to create one of today's *'big four'* cognac houses. (The other three were founded by merchants and foreigners: Richard Hennessy (in 1765) from Ireland; Jean Martell (in 1715) from Jersey, while Emmanuel Courvoisier (1835) was a Parisian – just as foreign in rural France!) Rémy Martin was also the only one to have his roots in the land. When he died at the age of seventy eight, in 1773, he left a thriving business to his grandson, another Rémy Martin. ■ Over the next two centuries, the firm of Rémy Martin continued to grow despite the political upheavals of the French Revolution, the loss of its main export markets during the Napoleonic wars, two world wars and German occupation. But for them as for everyone else in Cognac, the worst disaster of all came in the 1870's when phylloxera, a tiny aphid, struck. By 1880 the Cognac region was a desolate landscape of dead vines. Growers and merchants were ruined in their hundreds. For years afterwards, *'phylloxera'* was the threat hurled at naughty children. ■ But in some ways, phylloxera made Cognac the spirit it is today. It took more than ten years for the region to recover, and when it did it was thanks to a Texan, whose nursery at Denison on the Red River was found, in 1887, to have American rootstock (which was immune to the deadly insect) suitable for both the chalky Cognac soil and its white grape varieties. ■ Replanting was expensive and in some areas which had never produced very good wines it was not worthwhile. In that sense, overall quality was improved. The wholesale replanting of vineyards could also be done scientifically, and ordered rows, with room between for a horse-drawn plough, replaced the previous closely-grown, higgledy-piggledy vines. That, too, improved quality.

The Rémy Martin Centaur...
The Symbol of Taste

Fortunately, some Cognaçais combine several contradictory qualities which not only help them overcome disasters but also make the making of cognacs better. Cognac takes its time to distill and years to mature, so patience and farsightedness are needed. On the other hand, so is a shrewd head for business and a certain willingness to take risks. And when you are making something designed for export all over the world, to nations speaking many languages, you also need an instinctive flair for marketing. You need a logo with a strong global identity that doesn't offend one or more nationalities. ■ As long ago as 1870, Rémy Martin's great-great-grandson, Emile Rémy Martin, was pondering the problem. He decided on a Centaur. ■ Like centaurs themselves, Emile Rémy Martin was a stargazer – a keen astronomer – and a Sagittarius, symbolised by a centaur. Sagittarius could also be considered the birth sign of cognac since the distilling season starts in late November. Emile also knew his Greek mythology. ■ Centaurs are creatures, half man and half horse, said by many to symbolise man's dual nature as an intellectual creature (the *'head-in-the-clouds'* human half) and a physical animal (the *'feet-on-the-ground'* horse half). Sensuality vies with passion. Centaurs were also acolytes of Bacchus, the god of wine. ■ To Emile, the centaurs' contrasting combination of qualities were also characteristic of cognac: strength (begun in the earth and ending on the palate); mystery (the alchemy of the double distillation process), and ambiguity (its rusticorigins but sophisticated maturity). ■ Rémy Martin's Centaur is Chiron, celebrated for his wisdom and healing abilities and the friend and mentor of Achilles. It also seemed apt to Emile that Chiron's father was Chronos, making him the son of Time

itself: a commodity much needed for making fine cognacs. ■ Emile Rémy Martin had other good reasons for choosing this particular Centaur to represent his company, for Chiron is a visual metaphor of Rémy Martin cognacs in all their contradictory guises from the vineyard to the glass.

The Rémy Martin Centaur awakens all the senses to the taste of excellence...

Emile Rémy Martin's choice proved to be an inspired one, not least a century later, in the markets of the Far East. Not only is cognac itself regarded as an aphrodisiac there, but the Chinese, unable to pronounce many Western names, have no trouble asking for retinomah – a glass or bottle of 'man-headed horse' cognac. And was it just coincidence that Emile Rémy Martin – though he almost certainly didn't know it – was born in the Chinese year of the horse? ■ Of course, during the last two centuries, Chiron himself has changed to keep up with changing times. And yet he is still quintessentially himself. Certainly, as Rémy Martin has gone from strength to strength, he has lost none of his abilities. Rather they have been renewed, refined and enhanced. ■ His big change came in 1966 when he emerged more vital than ever: more of a thoroughbred from the waist down but with the head and broad, muscular torso of a man who was a regular at the gym and worked out with weights. This Chiron's front hooves rear high into the air, looking as though he is about to leap into the heavens and, instead of aiming an arrow at the ground, as he had originally, he is now ready to fling a javelin skywards. ■ Today, Rémy Martin is indisputably one of the two most important players in the cognac market: a position the Centaur celebrates with panache as he carries his messages of tradition and vision; wisdom and adventure, finesse and taste to the four corners of the globe.

The Perpetuation of Taste...

Cognac is a mysterious spirit in some ways. No-one is really sure why it came into being, and the 'inventor' of distillation, the technique for making cognac, is lost in the mists of history. ■ Yet in other ways, it is straightforward. Technically, anyone who can grow grapes can distil their wine into brandy. They can grow the same grape varieties, distil in the same way and age their spirit in identical barrels for the same number of years. But they will never be able to produce cognac – and not just for legal reasons. ■ Everything starts with terroir, that untranslatable word which combines the character of the soil, rainfall, sunshine, wind, temperatures and the people who understand these, to give even a tiny region its own distinct identity. ■ In Cognac, the soil is chalky and crumbly, especially in the crus, or regions, of Grande and Petite Champagne. This porous soil can absorb and hold rainfall, releasing it gradually to the vines, but its

chalkiness also dictates the types of grapes which will grow well in it. In Cognac, these have varied over the centuries but today there are three main varieties: Ugni Blanc, Colombard and Folle Blanche. Ninety percent of the vineyards are planted with Ugni Blanc. ■ The rain, as they say in Cognac, falls often but in small amounts, making it wetter than most of France. But the summer days are long and every visitor notices their special light. The sun is never harsh but seems to be filtered through the sky with a gentle luminosity. The chalk soil reflects the light up to the vines and the combination produces a gradual, but regular, ripening of the grapes. ■ The whole region, but again especially Grande and Petite Champagne, benefits from a special microclimate. Not only does it lie right at the border between

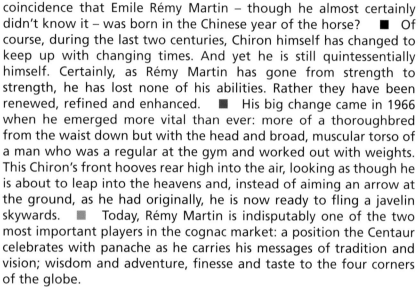

northern and southern France but its gentle hills cradle it and protect it from the harsher weather of the Atlantic Ocean to the west and the mountains of central France to the east. So the temperature is generally warm and rarely goes to extremes. ■ This unique combination has proved perfect for producing cognac. Nowhere else in the world has the same blend of geography and weather and while they may produce a brandy, it will always lack the finesse and complexity of a good cognac. ■ The gentleness of the landscape and the weather (and 'gentle' is the word everyone applies to all aspects of the region as well as its climate) produces grapes that press into wine which is both acidic and low in alcohol. Not what you want in a glass of white wine. But the levels of both acidity and alcohol are ideal for distilling. ■ Like all other cognac companies, Rémy Martin buys most of its spirits from independent growers who must respect the company's stringent quality charter. Unlike most, however, for over fifty years it has only bought from the Grande and Petite Champagne regions – the two areas which produce the finest, most intense spirits – where it works in partnership with almost two thousand growers who all abide by its quality charter. ■ The grapes are crushed and fermented for two weeks before distilling into a clear spirit known as eaux-de-vie. The most aromatic come from wines distilled on their lees (their natural sediments) though the law does not demand this. The lees create the distinctive rich, complex overtones only present in the best cognacs. They also give a greater range of aromas, texture and smoothness to the final cognac. At Rémy Martin all wines aredistilled on their lees. Twenty-five pounds of grapes produce about ten quarts of wine which, in turn, distill into only two pints of eaux-de-vie. ■ The double distillation process demanded by law can be nerve-wracking. Distilling starts in mid-November and must be completed by 31 March of the next year. During these months you could be blind and deaf and still know you were in Cognac: the rich, grapey aromas from the hundreds of distilleries suffuse the atmosphere. For the distiller, however, it's the liquid dripping from the stills that matters. ■ Some, like Rémy Martin, only distill in the traditional small alambic charentais which holds 2,500 liters (just over 660 gallons) since this has proved to be the size which gives the greatest taste benefits to the eaux-de-vie, concentrating its aromas, much as a small saucepan reduces broth to a richer glaze than a stock-pot. Also, eaux-de-vie produced in batches are much superior to those produced by continuous stills.

■ Since the first distillation takes ten to twelve hours and the second, twelve to fourteen, and the still must be thoroughly cleaned after every distillation, the distillery works twenty four hours a day, with the distiller often sleeping on a cot-bed on the premises. ■ The alambic charentais, as its name suggests, is unique to Cognac and they have a magic of their own. Made of copper – and always richly gleaming – they have changed little in three hundred years. The onion-shaped pot still which holds the wine, is firmly bedded in brick above an open fire. Originally wood was used, but today, the heat generally comes from natural gas: electricity is out because the law decrees the use of flames. ■ As the wine heats, the alcohol vaporizes and rises through a *'swan's neck'* which funnels it down into a swirl of pipes contained in a cooling chamber filled with cold water. As it descends, it condenses into liquid to emerge as a milky brouillis, or low wine, with an alcohol content of about thirty-percent after the first distillation. The second distillation produces a clear spirit, la bonne chauffe, at seventy-percent alcohol by volume. ■ But not all the eaux-de-vie can be used. The first part in both distillations will be too harsh and the last part too weak. It is the distiller's art to know just where to stop and start. Of course, today's distiller has instruments to help him but most rely just as much on sight, taste and smell as on science. ■ All new eaux-de-vie are sampled to decide their future life. At Rémy Martin a team of master tasters, men and women of multiple skills, make the decisions. Each possesses the nose and palate to predict the tastes of the future. Their consensus guarantees quality and consistency. To see them at work, either when buying or putting together the components of a final blend,

which can contain hundreds of eaux-de-vie (Rémy Martin's best-selling V.S.O.P contains two hundred and forty), is to watch a great art, with each eaux-de-vie making its own mark on the taster's palate and memory bank. ■ The crystal-clear eaux-de-vie begin their ageing process in new oak barrels. As they mature into cognac, they will be transferred to older barrels. The wood can come from the Limousin or Tronçais forests and the choice is important for the wood will imbue the spirit with tannins, color and subtle flavors. Eaux-de-vie from Grande and Petite Champagne – which are the only ones Rémy Martin buys – require longer ageing than those from other crus to reach their full aromatic complexity. So only wood from eighty-year old Limousin oak trees is used because it has the wide grain needed to allow the complex tastes of long-maturing cognacs to develop fully. ■ A visit to the tonnellerie, or cooperage, is fascinating and the barrels are almost as important to the final taste of the cognac they contain, as the actual distillation. Like the barrels the cooperage also makes for Château Petrus, Krug Champagne and Robert Mondavi Opus One, they are made from split oak, which are stacked outdoors to season for at least three years so that any bitter elements can leach out. The classic size holds 350 liters (a little less than 100 gallons): this has proved itself over centuries to produce the best balance between eaux-de-vie's initial, fruity aromas and the subtle aromas it will absorb from the wood. ■ It takes ten years to become a master cooper and seeing them at work you know why. No nails or glue can be used. So the thirty two staves that make up each barrel must be fitted together perfectly to prevent leakage. They are first shaped into a 'lampshade' with hoops and then 'toasted' over an open fire of oak chips to help release the flavors and aromas, especially vanilla, which the young eaux-de-vie will absorb on their way to maturity. The 'lampshade' must then be moistened just enough to give it the flexibility to form its final barrel shape. Tops and bottoms are made from oak planks sandwiched together with reeds and fixed with wooden dowels. When attached to the barrel, they are sealed with a flour-and-water 'putty'. It is reckoned that two barrels represent a day's work for one man and, at around $600 each, they are a major investment. ■ Ageing takes time! Once filled, the barrels are stacked in cellars – though in Cognac, most of these are above ground. The forty two ageing cellars of Rémy Martin shelter six thousand barrels each, containing the largest stock of Fine Champagne Cognac in the world. Made of the local limestone they – like every building holding cognac in barrels – are coated by a fine layer of black fungus. This is torula cognacensis, which thrives on the vapors that evaporate through the barrels over the years. This natural evaporation is rather romantically called 'the angels' share' and usually amounts to three percent a year. For Rémy Martin, that means the entire contents of 6,000 barrels disappear every year. ■ The temperature and humidity of the cellars are carefully controlled as the cognac itself moves from younger to older barrels as it ages. How long that takes depends on the decision of the tasting team which regularly samples the stock, deciding which cognacs should be blended when – and for which of its brands it should be reserved. Every style of cognac has a minimum age laid down by law: for example, the cognacs blended in any V.S.O.P (Very Superior Old Pale) should be at least four years old, though Rémy Martin age their cognacs considerably longer than required so that they mature to their full potential which, in turn, gives added length to their aftertaste. ■ Cognac does not improve indefinitely in barrels: thirty to forty years is the maximum for most fine cognacs. But exceptional ones can improve for another fifty and reach their century. Once blended and bottled, there will be no further evaporation, so the cognac will never change. ■ Time, as we know, is money but Rémy Martin believes that the resulting richness of taste is worth the wait – and the extra cost. Taste, taste and more taste: this is the promise fulfilled by Rémy Martin in all its cognacs. Their floral, fruit and spice notes as well as their richness, complexity and length all combine in a feast of flavors and a memory of lasting pleasure.

Capturing the Spirit of Taste...
From Barrel to Bottle

There are few givens in blending cognac but nothing is haphazard. Each desired style will be a blend of spirits of various ages. But a decisive element in ageing is the cru, from which the spirit comes.

The slowest to mature and which also have the greatest potential for development come from Grande and Petite Champagne. ■ As they mature, amazing transformations take place in the cool silence of the cellars. Unlike other spirits – all of which are distilled from grain and tend to come off the still as raw alcohol – new brandy eaux-de-vie has a floral, fruity aroma which hints at the promise to come. These, called the primary aromas, are the backbone of the spirit which will be fleshed out and colored by spicy nuances, the secondary aromas, absorbed from the barrels as they age. ■ All eaux-de-vie will be tasted regularly to chart their progress: some will reach their full potential in less than ten years; others can continue to mature for over fifty. The contents of each barrel will be different. And there are almost a quarter of a million barrels of varying ages at Rémy Martin. ■ The tasting team at Rémy Martin devote their working lives to tasting, day in and day out. They must bring to it a combination of skills: intuition, experience and, perhaps above all, a taste memory of the thousands of different eaux-de-vie. Actually, to call them tasters is something of a misnomer for, since ninety-percent of taste comes from smell, they use their noses much more than their mouths. ■ Vincent Géré, Master Taster, defines the styles of the Fine Champagne cognacs Rémy Martin makes and ensures that they are achieved and can be continued by the cellarmaster. Pierrette Trichet, the cellarmaster, decides and assembles all the component eau-de-vie needed for the blend. She is one of the very few women in the business at such a top position. ■ Together they compose each assemblage, or blend, as an artist uses a palette – in their case, a palette of hundreds of different eaux-de-vie rather than colors – to ensure continuity of style and consistency of taste throughout the range of cognacs. The team also, from time to time, 'invent' new harmonies. Their room is as much a library as a laboratory, though instead of books, the shelves are filled with samples of spirits from different sources and different years all kept for reference. How they achieve this is almost impossible for the layman to grasp. Marrying the different ages and types of spirit can only be done by people with deep knowledge of every aspect of cognac-making from the soil to the final blend.

The Taste Palette of the Rémy Martin Collection...

The cognac region has been delimited in 1909. ■ The six crus, or areas, from which cognac can be made have been defined by law since 1909. At about the same time, it was generally recognized that the finest cognacs come from eaux-de-vie made from grapes from the two central crus, Grande Champagne and Petite Champagne. ■ Only cognacs blended from these two regions and containing at least fifty-percent Grande Champagne can be called Fine Champagne Cognac. All Rémy Martin cognacs are blends from just these two top crus. They are also aged considerably longer than required by law. ■ The result is intensity of taste coupled with a silky smoothness; heady aromas coupled with delicate undernotes, and maturity coupled with liveliness. These characteristics distinguish all Rémy Martin cognacs.

Rémy Martin Grand Cru Cognac

Grand Cru stands at the top of the V.S (Very Special) category of cognacs that are made from one-hundred-percent Petite Champagne eaux-de-vie. Notes of wild flowers, crisp fruit, vanilla, honey and a hint of mint make an immediate impact on the palate. ■ It is a party person: lively, fresh, full of life and a good mixer – perfect for long drinks and cocktails as well as neat or on the rocks – an inviting, bright, attractive spirit to be enjoyed before, during and after meals. ■ Although cognacs need only be aged for two years for this grade of cognac, all those in Rémy Martin's Grand Cru have been aged from three to ten years. It represents the higher standard of V.S cognacs.

Rémy Martin V.S.O.P
Fine Champagne Cognac

Critics and connoisseurs alike agree that this is the benchmark of quality against which all other V.S.O.Ps are judged. Not surprisingly, it is the world's favorite – one in three of all bottles of V.S.O.P sold in the world is Rémy Martin – with its distinctive frosted bottle promising a consistently smoothblend of fifty-five-percent Grande and forty-five-percent Petite Champagne cognacs. ■ It is mature and supple with heady notes of violet and rose; ripe apricots and peaches, vanilla and hazelnuts. These ripe, aromatic flavors are contributed by eaux-de-vie which have been aged in oak barrels from four to fourteen years (none needs be older than four), making it the longest-aged V.S.O.P on the market. ■ To be drunk neat, on the rocks, or in classic cocktails, V.S.O.P also has enough facets and depth to partner the powerful punch of blue cheeses such as Roquefort, Stilton or Gorgonzola.

Rémy Martin 1738 Accord Royal

One of the most versatile of cognacs, 1738 Accord Royal commemorates the year in which Louis XV broke his own rule forbidding the planting of more vines in Cognac. He made an exception for Rémy Martin, recognising that the company would concentrate on quality not quantity in their eaux-de-vie. He was proved right and today 1738 Accord Royal recreates the rich, authentic, recognizably-different flavors of that time, using the original, closely-guarded method of production. Indeed, its upfront flavors led Vincent Géré, who describes the blend, to nickname it 'Mr More'. The four to twenty year-old eaux-de-vie in the blend are sixty-five-percent Grande Champagne. ■ The result is a structured cognac for connoisseurs, which can be enjoyed, accompanying a meal or on its own. Its notes of brioche, oak and candied fruits especially complement chocolate desserts and exotic fruits such as lychees. Served at room temperature 1738 Accord Royal is complex. Poured over a few ice cubes which enhance its fruity, floral notes, it stays bold and chocolaty..

Rémy Martin X.O Excellence

This Fine Champagne Cognac fully warrants its name with aromatic richness and complexity coming from cognacs aged from ten to thirty-seven years (the law demands no more than seven). Eighty-five-percent of the blend is made up of Grande Champagne cognacs. ■ The flavors dance in the mouth and the velvet texture and finesse linger long on the palate. Its memorable taste is strikingly fruity, reminiscent of ripe figs and juicy plums with undernotes of toffee and freshly-grated cinnamon. ■ The excellence and age of this blend with its myriad aromas and opulent richness demand that it be drunk neat though it loses nothing by being served slightly chilled or over ice. Try it with foie gras at the beginning of a meal and as an enhancement to a chocolate dessert.

Rémy Martin Extra

The quintessence of Fine Champagne Cognac, Extra contains ninety-percent Grande Champagne cognacs, all of which are twenty to fifty years old. It is elegant and refined with a harmony of taste that is an aesthetic luxury. ■ There are complex tones of saffron, sandalwood, walnut and nutmeg and the whiff of a cigar box. Indeed, Extra is a cognac to be enjoyed neat and/or with a good cigar. (Incidentally, cognac and cigars have a longtime association made fashionable in the nineteenth century when the then Prince of Wales, later King Edward VII, preferred to enjoy both in the company of the ladies after dinner, rather than sit for hours with the men over port.) ■ Distinct and exquisite, the intensity and subtlety, the concentration and fragrance of Extra deserves to be savored slowly.

Louis XIII de Rémy Martin,
Grande Champagne Cognac

Undoubtedly the ne plus ultra of cognacs – king of spirits and spirit of kings – containing over one thousand eaux-de-vie ranging from forty to one hundred years old. Aged in barrels which themselves are more than a century old, Louis XIII is the unique reward everyone deserves to give themselves at least once in their lives. ■ Each bottle represents the expertise of three generations of cellarmasters each of which is working for the future pleasure of their grandchildren and great-grandchildren. ■ A culmination of rare flavors – myrrh, candied fruit, passion fruit, honey and more – Louis XIII is an unforgettable experience, a supreme taste of perfection whose aromas give joy to the palate for over one hour. ■ This liquid symphony is preserved in an exquisite Baccarat crystal decanter, the faithful reproduction of a Renaissance original found near Cognac over one hundred and fifty years ago. Richly decorated with fleurs de lys, the symbol of French royalty, it evokes the sublime spirit within. To be sipped indulgently.

The Pleasures of Taste...
The Only Rémy Dinners- In The Pursuit of Excellence

The Only Rémy Dinners were conceived in a spirit of adventure. They are serious but should be fun. A brainstorming session at Rémy Martin's headquarters in Cognac came up with the idea of pairing their cognacs with food. Cognac is a distillate of wine, they reasoned, and whole books are devoted to pairing them. It was already known that cognacs make good friends with chocolate and coffee. And, although cognac is the perfect finish to a fine dinner, why should it be relegated to the end of the meal? ■ Why not, they thought, ask some of the world's top chefs to experiment to develop menus in which a cognac would work well with every dish? Naturally enough, they started in France and, naturally enough, there was some scepticism at first. But Rémy Martin made it clear right from the start that the chefs had carte blanche. ■ A few weeks into the scheme, and obviously expecting to be accused of heresy, a much-Michelin-starred chef called HQ. Could he, he asked nervously, try chilling the cognacs? 'You can put them in the freezer if you like', was the unexpected reply. So he did. (The alcohol prevents the liquid from freezing solid.) The results were exceptional and added yet more possibilities to be researched. ■ Some notable menus were created. But France is France and French food is still based on tradition. To really explore all the possibilities, Rémy Martin decided to go abroad. And where else but the United States where some of the most adventurous combinations of food are served and rules are made to be broken (or at least questioned)? The result, as everyone now knows, is of course our Volume One- The Spirit of Excellence by David Shaw the publisher of Bon Vivant (formerly First Impressions of International Dining), where 30 of the USA's premier Chefs were asked to successfully pair their celebrated signature dishes with the specifically matched Remy Martin cognacs. ■ The logical conclusion was to continue this wonderful concept with a further series covering restaurants of the top echelon around the globe. And thus The Art of Excellence was conceived. All of the chefs approached by David and who have taken up the challenge in this book are the best and most creative in the world. Rémy Martin congratulates them on their inventiveness and flair. Obviously, they have individually discovered some common themes: Lamb, foie gras, shellfish and blue cheeses all turn out to be spectacular partners of cognacs. But there is also a fascinating variety in the pairings, in some of which, the dish and cognac are complementary, while in others, their tastes contrast. Both are equally valid. ■ You can, of course, prove this for yourself by simply visiting the restaurants of these chefs when they present the *"Art of Excellence"* concept on their menus. But you will also want to cook many of these delectable dishes in these pages, so why not organize your own *"Art of Excellence"* dinner for a special occasion? The first thing to remember is that it should be fun and the chefs have done all the hard work for you, including choosing which cognac they think makes the perfect match with each dish. Do you agree with them?

Advice on the Pairing of Cognac with Food

It's well worth following Rémy Martin Master tasting advice on how to taste your way through the meal, whether ordered in one of the restaurants in this book or at your own dinner party. Both should be relaxed occasions but there are certain rituals, which will make them special and even more enjoyable. ■ As far as tasting is concerned, it is worth taking your time. A Remy pairing Dinner can feature a range of three cognacs. ■ *"First of all unwind". You will be tasting the best Fine Champagne cognacs alongside dishes specifically created for them. It is a voyage of discovery and one of the most exciting things is that, because*

each cognac is a blend of anywhere from two hundred and forty to seven hundred different eaux-de-vie, different notes or facets come to the fore at different times depending on what each is drunk with and even at which temperature – ambient, chilled or fresh from the freezer – it is served. The different reactions with different foods really do help you understand the complexities of aromas contained in any one Rémy Martin cognac." ■ For example, Franco Barone of Antonello in California and David Feau of Lutece, in New York, create their pairings with chocolate - a Chocolate Souffle Cake (Barone) and a Rock Glass Warm Chocolate Cake (Feau) paired with Extra. Azul's Michelle Bernstein, in Miami, is most adventurous with complex flavor combinations in her Chocolate Mole Painted Foie Gras and paired with chilled VSOP. In fact, here, it is interesting to see how many chefs have found successful pairings with one of Rémy Martin's cognacs. and meat. Foie gras, of course, makes several appearances ■ Elsewhere, an iced Rémy Martin V.S, with its hints of vanilla and violet, may be served with a ceviche of thinly-sliced scallops; a brochette of langoustines and monkfish with a saffron sauce is enhanced by the same note of saffron in Rémy Martin Extra served chilled; the ripe fruit flavors of chilled Rémy Martin X.O bring out the best in pigeon breasts spiced Chinese-style, while the same cognac, served at room temperature, shows that its rich cinnamon and hazelnut aromas stand up to a strong, aged hard cheese, and Rémy Martin's best-selling V.S.O.P brings the contrast of liquorice and the complement of apricots to a lemon meringue tart with apricot sorbet. ■ But back to your tasting. To get the most out of a Fine Champagne cognac, it's worth indulging in some ritual. First, look at the cognac. Many people think that the darker the cognac, the older it will be. But don't be fooled: this is not true. Swirl the glass gently and examine the traces, or 'legs', of liquid as they slide back to base. They should slip down limpidly. ■ "Slowly bring the glass to your nose", says Vincent Géré, "rather than your nose to the glass. As it approaches, inhale several times. As it gets closer, fruit and floral aromas will make their appearance. As the glass reaches the nose, spice notes will join them. Take the time to appreciate them as their emphases change. A good cognac will immediately release a pleasant freshness and balanced fruitiness. The mature cognac will also start to release the complexity of the aromas it has absorbed from the oak barrels: spicy notes with wood and vanilla overtones. ■ Now taste, in small sips allowing the cognac to spread out in the mouth towards the back where the most sensitive tastebuds live. The finer and longer the taste remains on the back palate, the better the finish. The amazing complexities of aromas and refinements of flavors in Rémy Martin's cognacs are like an explosion in the mouth. ■ Take your first taste of the dish in front of you and appreciate the complexities and harmony of its ingredients. Now you can combine sips of the cognac with bites of the food. Your palate will find it surprisingly easy to recognize a changing kaleidoscope of taste. A good pairing, like Rémy Martin cognacs, is always more than the sum of its parts, taking them to a higher level. All flavors are intensified and bring out the best in each other. Each of you at the table may – in fact, almost certainly will – have different opinions of the pairings. But that is as it should be. By the end of the meal, you will truly understand the meaning of our French phrase *"chacun a son gout'!"*

A GOOD MEA
HARMONIOUS A
AND AS WELL O
A NORMAN CAT

MUST BE AS
A SYMPHONY
ONSTRUCTED AS
HEDRAL.

FERNAND POINT,
RESTAURATEUR
AND WRITER

LIVING THE VERY HY LIFE-
THE COMFORT AND STYLE IN MY EPICUREAN ODYSSEY

APPETIZERS-AMERICA

San Francisco – dreaming….

…The mists were drifting over the skyscrapers of this eclectic architectural dreamscape they call San Francisco and this is where my story begins…. The usual shenanigans… car horns, bustle… traffic roar. All just echoes in my mind as peace and serenity could be observed with the Golden Gate… truly the icon of the America Dream… carrying so many each with hope and ambition… now standing silently… as the sun lowers its golden shades to welcome a fast falling night… ■ Suddenly the telephone sounds and ever its obedient servant, I dutifully pick up the receiver a voice pleasantly informs me that room service is on its way up… You can't beat the personalized touches these Park Hyatt people offer, be it DC, New York, Chicago or here in San Francisco …the food arrives piping hot with an excellent half bottle of Chardonnay… I lounge in a larger than average stylish armchair… enjoying the hi-tech décor as I indulge…California dreaming… I drift off into a sound sleep…

Chicago-More than Just Beef

…It has stopped raining. To the bump and squeal of the soft tires we land at O'Hare… It is just after dawn… the roads to the Windy City are not even awake, a commercial vehicle and taxi or two, but not much else… I see the odd street person wending their way home – if you can call it that… I thank God for my freedom and for my privilege in being able to make the best of my life. We enter a city just starting to throb with energy… .A jogger huffs and puffs past as we sit dawdling at the lights. Green, and we turn the corner into North Michigan, the Water Tower as important to Chicagoans as the Sears Building, dominates the tiny square… the Park Hyatt is a shrine to Art… The Lobby is a misnomer for it truly is a gallery, where proudly hang Chihuly, Rochter and Noguchi…This is no ordinary run of the mill 5 star excellence; it respects the individual and caters precisely for those needs. Conde Nast loves this hotel group, as do the rest of the travel press …and indeed so do the many celebrities, dignitaries and simple common folk like myself. The service… personalized and effortless… all the stresses and strains of travel immediately erased at the drop of a *"Mr. Shaw, welcome home!"*… ■ My view from my high-rise apartment (for that is what each suite is in this elegant Hotel) is of the aforementioned Water Tower and the edge of Lake Michigan just beyond, where all is now gently and eerily aglow in a halo of floodlighting. ■ My busy day over… I relax in sheer luxury, in my tent like Terry robe, after a relaxing hydro-aroma therapeutic bath, in a tub made for two… I listen to my favorite Cole Porter romantic ballad playing timelessly from the cutting-edge technology of a sound system that envelopes the room… Finally I am dressed, Black Tie and all, to do justice to the Art-Cuisine of the hotel's celebrated Chef, Sandro Gamba and the sheer pleasure of the architectural elegance that is so inimitably Nomi, its much-lauded restaurant. ■ Exquisite breads, impeccable wines, and just about some of the most inventive dishes in the USA and I am sated…Dinner over, I step out of the restaurant to sit on a brightly lit treetop terrace… I inhale the sights and scents of this windy ugly beauty called Chicago… I light up my Bolivar over my coffee and Remy and draw my first taste… And still the night is young … Some old acquaintances approach who should never be forgot and we laugh and share the odd tale… *"Let's wander the town!"* someone suggests, and soon we are alighting from the high-speed lift… past the Armani-clad security staff, the very souls of discretion, and onto a lively street. A horse and carriage pass, its occupants entwined in a lover's embrace, some girls come towards us, but not the ones we once used to know (thanks Al

Stewart). We flirt with them and then like passing ships we move on... we find a blues bar... Ah Muddy Waters never sounds so good until you're in the blue tones of this magnificent towering City... its old classical buildings imply its ruggedness... its stability... its strength. Chicago is gritty...it is majestic, it reeks of an eclectic culture not unlike my other favorite metropolises, New York, London and Paris... ■ It is now late and I make my way back to this home from home which the Park Hyatt surely is...I'm in love with its elegance, its hushed and so discrete overtones, so delicately understated... its appreciation of my two favorite subjects-art and cuisine... my oasis in my busy time in this great city... possibly in my life... On the superb *"sensesurround "sound system, Ella is still singing "…. under my skin, I've got you deep in the heart of me…"* –And so do you PH of Chicago!

Washington D.C.-People, Power, Politics, and Pabulum

I love trains... the clickety-click... the swaying of the carriages...the stop-start, *"hellos"..."goodbyes"*... of old faces gone and new ones arriving...a staccato in the heartbeat of life... and its ubiquitous bustle and hustle... conveying the arteries of commerce, carrying the arteries of human life…Then the slow, final rumble, heralding, not the end, but a nascent arrival in the capital's Union Station...in the heart of DC. A classic welcome to a classic city... steeped in tradition … elegantly attired like a night on the town. Awash with lights exposing the dark corridors of power... the center of all things Political… breaths of scandal behind hushed doors... secrets affecting the Nation's security, kept locked safely, so that America breathes and sleeps soundly tonight … Yet, it' s fun... it is enchanting… its one pace is ordered, as indeed was the Senate of Ancient Rome… Civilized and oh so classy… ■ The mighty Potomac flows-a case of still waters running silent... the ghosts of Watergate….running deep… Then I approach a majestic hotel... accommodating, elegantly attired staff-no doubt disciples of the charming, dapper Paul Pisarz, its stylish and so very human G.M. The Park Hyatt reflects food, taste and like its sister properties, it embodies style and Art from William Adair, Georges Braque, locals like Cushner, Davis and Downing, even a Brit or two like Hockney (a personal favorite) Matisse (another!), Picasso (a third)... all are alive and well at this most welcoming of establishments… ■ I feel like a King in his capital city, I'm allowed to feel as rich as Croesus, I feel indulged as I indulge... *"All part of the service sir!"* My suite... luxurious as big as a bowling alley, flowers... champagne...canapés from top culinary luminary Brian Metcalfe, whose famed Melrose and gourmet delights are still to be had. And the sting of some frenetic days, dealing with the odd *prima donna* now just a distant nightmare behind me, as I slowly unpack... the hot

shower in a marble bathroom-all glass and mirrors-I am human again! …And so to dinner… and my rendezvous with all thing quintessentially epicurean…Metcalfe is the Chefs' chef in this city that has surrendered to the French invasion... he sits comfortably with the likes of Richard, the late Paladin, Pangaud, and of course Washington's own Riz Lacoste... and boy can he cook… A better Pan-seared Scallops with white asparagus and black truffle vinaigrette I can not imagine, nor a heavenly Hazelnut Praline and Raspberry Fleur, wrapped in Chocolate and like the artists surrounding him, presented on a painted plate. …Shades of Picasso? ■ And still I hear the music... in my head, in my soul and in a Melrose, room-full with Jazz... Ellington… Goodman… Miller… ■ With so many fond memories, I look round and give the huge thumbs up to Paul, as the sleek limo draws away. I will be back… I muse and I am all smiles….

New York-a slice of the Big Apple

Station to station... great city to city... from the country's capital to the world's capital... New York-the epicenter of the arts, food, entertainment, culture... glamour... a thousand accents, colors and creeds ... the epitome of the melting pot... a fusion of some of the most brilliant minds in the universe... New York! New York! The city that will not cannot and never can sleep... A beer and a hamburger at dawn...a street life of streets... a grid where the heart is... the giant...no nonsense, tough guy, if you push you can get hurt, but only in your ego... for there is huge heart here, if you fall it will catch you, ask Trump, ask Leona, ask a City that held together during September 11th and its ghastly aftermath, and then the great Blackout... ■ And yet with some sadness, I find myself looking over the placid view of a silent Central Park... out of the faded elegance of the Stanhope on 5th Avenue. I sip my Manhattan Sour, as I listen to the sweet sound of the starlings...I am reminded of a fellow publisher, one of America's late sons... like a candle gone out in the wind of tragedy and reflect what JFK Jnr. did on his last night here... considering the fate of George or the happiness with his family wedding celebrations... ■ But I guess I am just being over-maudlin, for life has to go on like the never-say-die heartbeat of Manhattan. ■ I am now sitting out on a balmy August night watching the crowds wending their way past the Metropolitan Museum... So very New York,

and only in New York I spy a performance artist all diaphanous white... dancing like Isadora , free and unfettered... the earthy smell of the horses and carriages as they clatter through the slow moving traffic... ■ I can smell the hotdog stalls of National Hebrew reminding me of a favorite time when my darling idiot Son Adam used to squeak, "Dad I am hungry!" for the millionth time in under less than ten blocks. The Stanhope is the epitome of discretion and it reassures me, with its quirky yet oh so warm service. The rooms are clean spacious and stylish with gilt appointments and all swags and drapes and comfort just like my Mum's home back in South East London... The smell is one of familiarity and I can sleep easily and deeply tonight... But for now it's a Martini or three as I allow myself the luxury and abandon of intoxication, I can sing... I can dance... and here at this celebrated Hyatt institution, very much a part of New York life, I can indulge and have a smile or a laugh reciprocated by an indulgent wait-staff as I unhurriedly linger over my well-prepared early dinner... pouring over the City's news in the early edition of the Post.   ■ I am so looking forward to Saturday... a breakfast on the Terrace watching the early shoppers over my perfectly poached eggs and whole-wheat toast and my bottomless cup of coffee... And it is here that I can simply cross over the most famed street in the world 5th Avenue and get lost in the profusion of greenery that dominates Central Park where joggers and the world can pass me by... I am never alone... not at the Stanhope... not in New York...

Singapore... Lions and Bold as Brass Monkeys...
... Within the shade of the lazy jungle, the lion sleeps tonight..."

Stamford Raffles was a clever bloke... East India Company... a young entrepreneur of some ambition... taking care to develop British interests abroad especially in the Far-East... to establish political and economic presence... He basically founded Singapore... in 1819. ■ Funny thing is... I was born in Madras, a city founded by the East India Company and 12 months later my Dad a serving officer, with the British Army was posted to Singapore another Company city... ■ The Lion City.... An amazing eclectic city of a great English – speaking civilization , glass and concrete skyscrapers, a myriad accents and colors...a people of 4 million ... Islamic, Muslim, Hindu, Brahmin, Buddhist, and that so divine Eurasian... that exotic Singaporean mélange, rich tapestry of people, voices that will always be heard in this amazing democracy. Ancient Rome and Greece eat your metropolitan hearts out... this affinity with the number one... airport, airline busiest port...bunkering port...largest fountain and highest man-made waterfall... all from one energy source... its people! The magnificence of cultures and history, race and color and creed, reaching out to embody a national pride... bringing out the best in humanity... a tribute to this society's creative soul ... I am overwhelmed by the abundance of Deco... Deco, my timeless love, is everywhere , marrying in total harmony the equally stately and timeless colonial architecture of memsahibs, colonels, governors and kings..... Busy street, green and white taxis everywhere like a tide on a sandy beach, and even Beckham and Manchester United ...so much for iconoclastic imagery...I am free falling in this amazing past present and future... Lee Kuan Yew is a visionary genius for his first priority of commonwealth and good manners... low crime... zero unemployment... People work hard... but with an end to indulge... and indulged am I at a Grand Hyatt that, with all its Singaporean charm and hospitality welcomes, me home... ■ Sumptuous feast in the Mezza9, enjoying the island's characteristic eclecticism from a myriad origins, Japan, Britain, China Malaya India Holland USA... a feast for a returning adopted son... Even a prodigal son... for how sorry I am to have neglected this beautiful city for over 40 years... ■ The suite is really an apartment... I feel reckless as I sprawl on a king size bed... eating ramatans... my favorite type of lychee... I gingerly move my fingers around the prickles to get to the luscious fruit and I am reminded of the Botanical Gardens, where bold as brass monkeys would insolently scurry up to us to scrounge our pickings from the rambutan tree at the crest of the small grassy hill... The three televisions are all tuned into an English station, keeping me posted on the Big Match involving my beloved Arsenal, some thousands of miles away... ■ I think of my father, sadly now deceased and how he was immortalized after hitting an unbowed and undefeated innings of 42 runs...that humid day out on the Padang... Becoming part of the folklore of the Singapore Cricket Club...the Clubhouse overlooking the Padang... you can see two impish pipsqueaks scampering hither and thither... Magnolia ice cream bars rapidly melting in the hot afternoon sun... My memories stir up so many images...the historical Princess Elizabeth Hall dominates my thoughts ...immense neo Classic facades. A dramatic puissant backdrop to the thunder of cymbals and kettle drums and an orchestra with 100 voices in full throttle...I felt important then as with pride I heard my mother's compelling solos there and also for the BBC Forces Schools network radio... The open live-stock market was around by the Causeway that spanned between Singapore and Johore in Malaya... We used to picnic in Penang

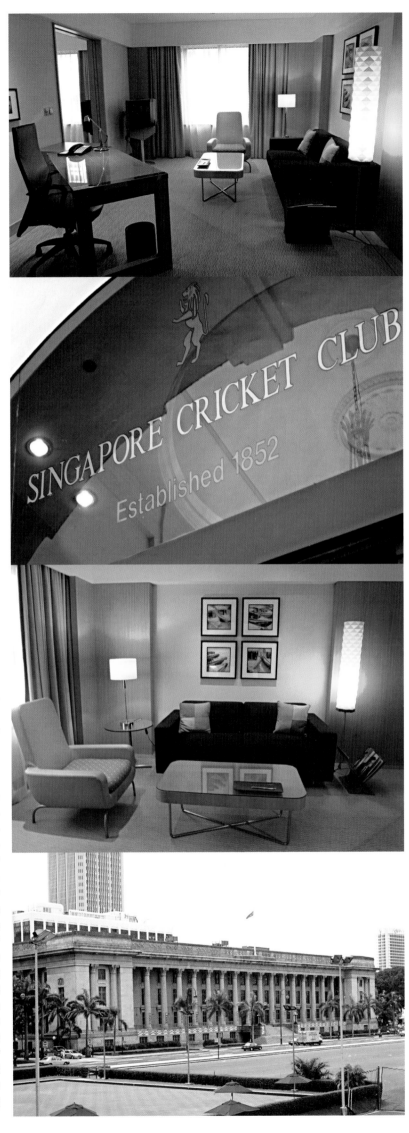

on the beach where, we would play with a tiny duckling which my flustered Dad, under immense pressure from two wailing infants, had to purchase from that same market... ■ I glance down at the lavish fruit bowl and the cheese board and crackers that the discretely efficient Guest Services have placed on my huge lacquered coffee table... The luxurious surroundings and such top-notch service make me smile appreciatively...and I wallow indulgently in all of it... ■ No surprises why they call it the Grand... staying here elevates the quality of life ...I have just soaked up all the goodness in a Jacuzzi, after a muscle relaxing massage at the Club Oasis... time for tea or, as I look at my watch... the sun going down... a cocktail or two in Scott's Lounge... where you

really do lounge... a lovely smiling cocktail hostess...lights my Romeo and Juliet cigar for me, with the same precise efficiency that my Goon Bay Smash is prepared. The light, refracting through belled glass windows, accentuates the timelessness of these surroundings... and all the while, the faultless smiling service goes on, without missing a beat. The credo here is to demonstrate job satisfaction at every opportunity... to enjoy your job... the combination of fun and hard work is probably alien to many Westerners-so much so that I wonder if back home, we really understand just what the word hospitality means...and what are we missing... Yet for now here at this so accommodating hotel, it is service with a genuine smile ... ■ The grandeur of a sweeping Deco inspired staircase is not wasted on me as I climb the steps to the restaurant and lounge complex that is quintessentially Mezza9... I see the open plan island theater kitchens, I see and experience the several different cuisine cultures of the unique entertainment concept Mezza9 - nine dining and lounge areas. Very apt... I am fascinated with the flair and activity... after a quick peruse at the gourmet patisserie and inhaling a Napeolon or three, I stroll into the split level lounge and Cigar bar where, enticingly, there is a generously sized humidor, displaying Cuban specialties of all gauges and lengths... Aah Winnie, wish you were here! And the Cheongsam-clad hostess...Such porcelain, silky, skin and grace .. Singapore is a very seductive town... ■ And my accommodations are quite exotic and serene... the Feng Shui and its cerebral monk who inspired the all embracing culture of well being... wrapping its becalming cloak

around me ... I enjoy the artistic nuances... modern art-some Picasso inspired, some from local brushstrokes. The room is all classic oriental touches...and more Deco...My Deco! Making my stay here so perfect ... I sink back into deep comfort.. The Bang and Olufsen system plays Porter and it all starts to get under my skin ...this hotel so deep in the heart of Singapore ... I nostalgically recall Change Alley and the urgent cries of the vendors, challenging you to find better or cheaper... the spice laden alluring smells of the old Esplanade at night ... perspiring young lads rush back and

forth from the horseshoe shaped complex... brown arms outstretched, bearing platters of the indigenous and traditional Satay, marinated to perfect spicy sweetness ...exotic... entrancing... appetizing ... unforgettable... my mouth waters in reaction to this vivid first taste of Singapore... ■ The cheery optimism in the bartender's voice gently intrudes my thoughts, *"Another Tiger Beer Mr. Shaw"*-Ah! I reflect... a beer of true character... and complicated... unlike anything that you have ever imbibed, or experienced ... I look through the huge floor to ceiling windows of the split level bar in this splendorous property, watching a Singapore, the Lion city, in its rush hour home ... the sounds and the activity taking on a different tone and mood... ■ And yet one has to marvel at Singapore, this universally celebrated Garden City of Asia, a florid abundance of trees, vegetation and flowers from a thousand shores, for below the surface, there is this sophisticated business acumen that so easily adds strength to its people... truly a case of East not just meeting West, but embracing in a cultural coupling. ■ 1972. Over thirty years have passed since its doors were opened and its reputation is international now as it was then. The lobby I relax in, is in effect a shopping mall that would impress the Beemer out of a Californian... cigar shops. The aromas reach out for you like a genie from Aladdin's lamp... a chocolatier... and a patisserie. Rivaling each other for your confections. I stroll over to the sound of a pianist ...delicate touch on the black and white... I like the easy style and the easy attitude... just a pot of tea.... Darjeeling, some biscuits and some finger sandwiches...no problem... the tea turns to a cocktail... nice martini. I am stirred by the great sounds from the keyboard... the gentle tinkle of polite conversation ...not too raucous, not so soft that the ambience lies mute... but then I love to people-watch and even the gentle purring lightly staccato conversations amuse me. I smile and thank a totally indulgent wait staff... I stare up to the grand balustrade that dominates the soaring lobby, where I spy some very exotic people dressed to the nines obviously *en route* to boogie the night away in the underground exclusive Brix night club-a labyrinth of bars and themes; wine... whisky... and music...rock on baby... listening to the band rocking the Casbah unto the early hours of the morning... I join the party and mingle with an eclectic crowd... a girl smiles a second time at me... as she glances sideways at others ... just a lady working the joint...escaping her lonely world to a place where she feels warmth and the pulse of the energetic, animated crowd.... the night moves on at a relentless pace. I emerge; breathing in the nascent day, tasting the early mists on my lips... a taxi and a rickshaw swish past ... the

brilliant lit forecourt of the Grand is like a beacon showing a world traveler the way to the heart of this great city... into its welcoming arms...

Hong Kong's city of Ghostly Equilibrium

"Non rien de rien, non Je ne regrette rien, ni le bien qu'on m'a fait, ni le mal tout ca m'est bien egal"

...Piaff, the little Bird...I arrive in and leave this city of ephemeral memories of past, present and future, with the same no regrets...just that song now forever in my heart... ■ My story really starts on a hot humid late afternoon. I am amazed at the size of a modern structure and a throbbing airport that welcomes so enthusiastically, the curious and commercial to this teeming city...I find true love in a city, with its patterns of streets, of sweet incense, of song-birds calling out the morning dawn ... of kings and snakes...of religions and relics...of ghosts and memories from the Opium wars...Vasco Digamma and Portuguese peddlers. A magical Macaovian mystery tour of its streets of myriad merchants. The canton and its legacy... Beijing... of teeming streets and noisy traffic... of opium dens... General Gordon...Shanghaied... willingly, on my slow boat to Chinese mysteries... inscrutable... a vibrant performance and the clash of cymbals announcing the ritual Dragon Dance... hand made suits in 2 days-a shirt while you wait...hand-stitched...the unique skills of sweatshop endeavor...a sad irony ... Modern day marveling at the phenomenal skyline... dwarfing a harbor of steamers, junks, boats, fisherman...the garish hues clashing with the sleek... a mish-mosh of Harbour-life... the ebb and flow that carries man on his worldly voyage. ■ And Deco... The power of the 30's... artistically, politically, socially, culturally and architecturally... imperial nights of black ties and martinis...snooker... gin and tonics in the sun that never set...

And cool... so suave...style... Girls in the seductive severity of the Cheongsam... ■ And a welcome at this Grand Hyatt awaits you like a returning Emperor, for that is how you feel. ...From the first greeting and an entourage of personnel, as they shower you with greetings and salutations. The overwhelming feeling of generosity of spirit is hard to ignore... Polish and servility, but of the proud sort... And what a hotel... A shrine to deco and clinging to the heady days of that magnificent period when the mysteries of China found an artistic bedfellow with the emerging eclecticism of Art deco...A hotel for all seasons of history and ever so posh...and so...Grand!...Imposing its will and style on the surrounding glass and steel superstructure. Elegance, shining like a beacon amidst the nightly performances of neon. ■ Highly accomplished service ...so very discrete... a diplomat's dream, a veritable statesman's temporary residence... or just surrounding magnificent splendor in which to rest your weary businessman's head... There is an assurance here of handling the most difficult and demanding of guests-making it truly a *"celebrity"* hotel, where the word *"impossible"* is impossible! From the elegant General Manager, Robert Barker, whose warmth, humor and humanity, quickly forges a lasting camaraderie with me, as we imbibe our Kirs Royal seated at the celebrated Champagne Room, down to the Boss-attired bell hops, there is an air of quiet confidence and understated humor that denotes an ability to handle the sublime to the ridiculous, with all the aplomb of an international ambassador, for are they not? And still this place seems so very British with its manifest traditions *"A spot of Tea, Dear Boy... Darjeeling or Earl Grey?"* ... *"always a pleasure old boy..."*...a wonderful mixture of old world civility, Eastern hospitality and cutting edge technology, spanning the void of time and geography... A place to enjoy the creature comforts of a modern age, imbued with old-fashioned kindnesses and courtesy and...luxury! luxury! luxury! ■ I sit talking in my suite-ersatz apartment, the former would be a gross understatement... with my associates, musing over my first impressions of this magnificent property and this historic city... Choice is a key note in staying here... dine at any of their restaurants, each enjoying an internationally acclaimed reputation or luxuriating in the health spa, or even... perhaps after a goodnight's sleep in the imperial-size bed, taking the plunge in the oceanic dimensions of their swimming pool! ...As they used to say, *"such wonderfully agreeable accommodations..."* ■ Hong Kong is still so British... there seems almost a silent popular vote to not let go so soon...perhaps they may never let go... indeed why change this cultural melting pot? At least not its life style that works so harmoniously with life at this hotel. The streets at night are like a maze... but you always can find your way home...thanks to a basic command of a language that is never lost, no matter the varying dialect! This economy is alive and well, as mirrored by the type of resident this establishment attracts... celebrity... diplomats and even a David Beckham, as he bends the rules and takes a night out with this magnificent Real Madrid team...people stand in awe and hero worship... he ventures into warm, mysterious sepia, timeless tones of the Hyatt's star turn, the Champagne Bar... the singer entrances a rapt audience with the husky spiciness of a throaty voice that perhaps may remind him of his beloved Posh back in England...He enjoys the music and claps enthusiastically...but to her, he is just another handsome face in a crowd, as she dreams of Toulouse and her loved one so far away... *"Under my skin... deep... in the heart... of me ..."* *"Night and Day... you are the one..."* ■ She walks with a thirties poise and wears a forties, face but all I see, is this ghostly timeless creature with a siren's voice ...my reserve cannot hold me as slowly...deeply... I am drawn in... I see Dietrich and hear the blue notes of this plaintiff's angel's voice... I close my eyes to this ... a compelling time warp and a tribute the oh so longed for days of style... and for many of us, she is our *Chanteuse*... we are under her spell and cannot forget or let go... ■ I have a late meeting with the new chef of Grissini the hottest restaurant in town... I make my apologies to my acquaintances ... I insist on offering her a flute of Veuve Clicquot ... for the sake of good music and beauty and for past legends.. *"Merci Monsieur, mon plaisir!"* This is my first visit to Hong Kong and I want time to stand still for ever as I feel something has happened... aah Jason... you got away... but not I... have gone back so many years, as I listen to her plaintiff songs of love... her silhouette against this backdrop of stunning Deco, our Deco...and so my Pan-Asian love affair takes another turn...this time...the Chanteuse...with Marlene Dietrich's eyes... ■ The Chinese have such a way with food and of course Hong Kong is the home of Cantonese cuisine and a firm favourite with the Western palate... I sit and linger over my Jasmine tea, savouring my earlier samplings of this hotel's remarkable restaurant with a memorable address- One Harbour Road and I have to appreciate the ambiguity of the name, as I gaze through the panoramic windows, with the dramatic view of a magnificent harbour and it is one breathtaking view...and one heck of a harbour! The connotations of its *"number one"* are not lost on me...the number one Cantonese Restaurant in Hong Kong... an interesting premise... and a prestigious enough address... ■ ...My suite where we sit relaxing, with the fireworks exploding in a wonderful astral display of hues and shapes... a dramatic incendiary kaleidoscope...like children, we *ooh* and *aah!* And of course, although we should be content with an excellent Rose Laurent Perrier... supplied courtesy of Guest Services (now how did they

know I liked Rose?) we gorge ourselves with black figs and oh so sinful handmade chocolates…sweet dreams are made of this… ■ They are soccer crazy here… and yes I must shout it from the rooftops-I am too! And it's so gratifying to be able to keep track of the big game from three different TV sets…I am spoiled almost rotten…I smile, as I watch, soaking in my tub made for two, *"no candles tonight…Josephine"*…or lolling on my king size bed… or, as we are now, in a very stylish eclectic drawing room, … ■ I could run a Murdoch size publishing empire from here… considering all in room business facilities…fax, laptop terminals… copier…several phones-all with message-options and prompts…full sound and visual system…and in-room E-mail connectivity. And a Service par excellence, that is unobtrusive, but ready to hear the slightest whisper. ■ And above all, there is choice after choice…enough does not exist here… Seemingly a land flowing with the milk and honey…One Harbour Road and Grissini… all glass and chrome, dress up posh, and savor warm aromas from the famous breadsticks…and the brilliant Cucina Italia of the new kid in town…as he stays firmly in my picture…cooking up the proverbial storm… ■ In my travels, as I embrace this wonderful life, most hotels in a 5-star category boast only one genuine world class restaurant, but what impresses me, as I continue my Epicurean Odyssey, is the culinary excellence of this hotel's restaurants and the variety which in itself is a mirror on the diversity of Hong Kong. I reflect on this as I contemplate sampling the Japanese delicacies of Kaetsu…where I imagine the freedom cries of a running deer (the basis of its name) …of haute cuisine tempura and sushi, sake and friends…new ones and those I seem to have known for a hundred years… And the Grand never loses the politesse of its imperial stylings…the old courtesies, perhaps not politically correct…but frankly my dear-I don't give a damn! I delight in both the company of the ladies after dinner, as much as sitting for hours with my fellow bon vivants and the old brigadiers, over port and perhaps, a cognac or two…Distinct and exquisite, the intensity and subtlety, the concentration and fragrance of an Extra, over my Bolivar cigar deserves to be savored slowly…like this hotel…of pedigree…of diversity… of choice, like Hong Kong!

Tokyo-The sun also rises… in a city of contrasts.

The reception is as ever impeccably civil. But today's younger set has managed to retain their elder's civility with an impish hint of humor. The limo stands before us, its 5.0 liter engine quietly purring, the chauffeur waiting patiently, as I *"there… there…"* a tearful colleague, whose bag has not as yet made an entrance with the rest of the motley crew of baggage, each taking its turn to be retrieved by anxious passengers, in much the same way as parents wait anxiously for the child to emerge from the mêlée of kids, all shapes and sizes, on the first day of school term… having passed him a Kleenex, I then discuss the problem and the case of the missing …case, *da da da dum-a* "who dunnit" - and on our first day in Tokyo… there are no thieves here…not in this city of contrasts…only foreign misconceptions…Pity Charlie Chan was not around…but then, this is, likewise, not San Francisco. The Hyatt chauffeur is, with the usual Japanese stoicism, unfazed by this major tragedy. He dials into a concerned Malcolm Thompson, a very dear friend and General Manager of the Park Hyatt Tokyo…*" No, Thompson San. They were late… collecting the baggage…and one has gone missing…"* My colleague impetuously breaks away *"I want to go home!"* he wails. *"No, no, no!"*…I insist that everything will be fine and the bad man who took his belongings will be made to return them… especially as over my distraught, weeping, colleague's shoulder, I spy a similar case sadly encircling, the now very lonely, carousel…the case of the missing case, in fact, has turned out to be a case of mistaken cases… ■ If nothing else, apart for its wonderful sense of common courtesy and culture, civility, a devotion to architecture, art, fashion and …cooking, Japan has unquestionable efficiency. If there is a *"cock-up"*, they do not point the finger like we do back home … they simply fix it. ■ I try to reassure my colleague, and simply say, *"Let these people sort it out…"* And boy, are these Park Hyatt people good. Not surprising, when you consider that so many top pop stars, sports personalities, musicians, Hollywood A-list types and statesmen, make this their residence of choice, when in this exciting, intriguing city of contrasts… ■ *"Fancy hotel key ring"*… I muse… just your regular Tiffany… but this is not flash… this is just par for the attention to detail that the Hyatt has here. Towering over the rest of a highly affluent and busy Shinjuku-ku area…the view is as thrilling as are the experiences…appreciate where East, with all its mysteries and cutting edge hi-technology, meets our laissez-faire culture of the West… ■ I am in a maudlin pensive mood as the limo sweeps regally into the forecourt of the Hyatt's pride and joy… A must for the discerning, and having only 71 elegant suites, it is boutique hotel in every sense. . Indeed, one is treated with great personal attention, as if purchasing a 50 karat diamond from Tiffany…there is no check-in, a senior manager accompanies you to your room and over a welcoming drink and canapés, enters you into the system, in this case, after old pleasantries have been exchanged, with my old friend Malcolm Thomson, an ultra professional General Manager (in my book there are three top echelon Hoteliers, one of them Caesar Ritz, is of course deceased, but the

other two still reign supreme...Dr Natale Rusconi, and...Malcolm) I find ourselves in a wrap around condo (you can forget suite or even apartment) with the added Manna-an abundant choice of his personally chosen wines... flat screen TV (three), trampoline size bed, cavernous bathrooms, business systems and a dressing room and a view of the old Buddhist temple and the ghostly silent Mt. Fuji...and all around, as far as the eye can see, the myriad shapes and colors of the spectrum called Tokyo. *"So Malcolm...tell me about that sitcom show in Britain..."* I mischievously enquire. He won't fall for this usual *"Mickey-take"*, but without dropping his serious look (actually his eyes twinkle constantly and always with much amusement and humor) *"So David tell me how is the book project going-the foie gras at the New York Grill is better than ever. Matthew is cooking out of this galaxy... and try that canapé..."* He gestures... *"it has smoked eel-your favorite..."* And on the banter goes...all with the wonderful intent to relax you and let you inhale the serenity that is embroidered into this property...a calm and order that serves as an ode to the profusion of art and objects d'art that are so synonymous with the Park Hyatt... ■
A quick shower and a change of clothes...And it's off to the topper-most of this monumental complex, where I can sit enjoying the sophisticated company of a Tokyo on the razzle in the New York Grill and listen to the band playing...blues and jazz ... the girl can sing a bit... but I wonder how is her Piaff or Dietrich. My mind wanders through the bluesy haze of my cigar smoke and look through the amber of my iced Rémy ...through the glass ...looking... searching for the face that redefined the 40's and a charisma that dominated the room. And invade my oh so very private thoughts. ■ *"Hello mate!"* a gentle slap on my back and there ,grinning, is my mate, Bret Patterson, surely

one of the most influential chefs in Pan-Asia and highly respected internationally, both by the critics and his contemporaries... The New York Grill has to be and indeed is, on of the world's best for dining, for three reasons, the great combo of Matthew Crabbe and Bret Patterson, the spectacular view and an ambience bar none... energy pulses throughout this room...if serenity prevails on the other floors, then up here the closer to heavens you get, the greater the animation and vitality. But it is energy with all the muscle of an Aston-Martin Superleggera-pure class and indisputable quality. ■ This is more akin to a supper club, but there is the super, hugely watch - able and immensely entertaining performance of a talented brigade of chefs, as they follow one brilliant act after another, to the thunderous applause of a loyal set of aficionados... *"Good trip?"* the Kiwi enquires, as he joins me ... it has been a long time and the friendship and camaraderie is as strong as ever... He is a good bloke and an even better cook. I contemplate the dinner I will enjoy ... a degustation par excellence, as Matthew with legerdemain magic delivers incredible dishes that arguably would eclipse an Escoffier! ■
We chat until the piano lid is slowly closed and the last mike stand is dismantled, people are still slowly moving out, lovers arms entwined, friends, chatting, smiling, laughing ... and a good time is being had by all... I stroll with Bret out of this restaurant's spectacular entrance, past the huge glass encased wine cellar. I am still amused with Japan's obsession with Baseball and New York, as depicted by the huge colorful murals that dominate the cavernous dining room. ■ The New York Grill and bar underlines the status of this great hotel and it doesn't get any better than this, a trip to Tokyo and a hotel par excellence and an ever-continuous procession of *"Hy-notes"* at

this Hyatt. ■ Venturing out at daytime to take in some business and catch up with my sightseeing...Tokyo is a wonderfully confusing contradiction of terms. Truly my city of contrasts...And despite the bustle of this ultra-modern metropolis, there is this wonderful feeling of order and correctness! We wait in vain for the usual rush hour of territorial blasts of the horn. Morning, noon and night we are constantly reminded of just how this society leads the way in serenity and simple respect for others. We need to look at ourselves and wonder how we have let things slide for so long. No matter, we could become quite introspective, but we are here to inhale the pulse of this vibrant tale of two identities, busy and focused by day, humorous and relaxed at night. We encounter the boardwalks hoardings signs...Beckham still "rules OK" here in Tokyo as we see clones proudly displaying Mohawks, braids and D'Artagnan goatees and mustaches...and lights of the fashionable Ginza, the neon, rich, animated, and exciting with color and foreign signs and the beat of the ubiquitous karaoke bars, but everywhere and always-welcoming. ■ It is 8.00am, I am down early mulling over my English newspaper "the Times of London" with my poached eggs (perfectly cooked in 2.45 minutes) just a bit runny in the middle so I can dip my toast points, black figs and Ceylon Tea... ■ The Girondole, where I am breakfasting on the 41st Floor is typically French – relaxing and romantic, with a fascinating focal point of black and white photographic studies, not unlike those French masters, Bresson and Doisneau, by international artist Vera Mercer, depicting a *café society du monde*, surrounding the upper walls of the main split level dining area. It is quiet and the conversations are decidedly muted... in many ways it reminds me of the power breakfast rooms that were so proliferate in early 80s New York. Not many celebs today I think, although... is that Angelina Jolie over in the corner... looking so natural with two other companions...indeed it is...I won't bother her. ■ *"Ah, Tiger....*

Premium Sake… served perfectly at room temperature .." … "I love you too Bondo San…" (From "You only Live Twice.") It is lunchtime and the Kozue Restaurant on the 40th Floor-styled in true Japanese tradition-is alive and very well and buzzing with business types, who sit in magnificently formal groups, discussing the yen over the excellent tempura and sashimi, presented by Chef extraordinaire Ken Ooe. His lunchtime clientele tends to be mainly Japanese, enjoying the signature Bento Box. I make a note to perhaps try dinner here and enjoy the contrasting casualness of more relaxed well-heeled international crowd...It is 5.45 am. The fish market is fascinating. There is much movement and activity, but not much noise, surprisingly. Again, good manners dominate this workplace...men slosh around in gum boots with purpose...a traffic cop, like something out of a Jacques Tatti movie, whistles and blows, with much drama and enthusiasm... barrows, laden with Jaws-size tuna, rumble past as I nimbly step out of the way of a motorized trolley. The market workers slice and dice eel, skate, barramundi, salmon, shark, swordfish and all things fishy. Eels are held with great panache before being gutted… blood and water mix, where oil and water cannot… and yet is all so clean … ■ The chef is a great sport. At his invitation, we find ourselves jumping in a cab and heading to Tokyo fish market. We wander through the narrow lanes watching the professional buying the day's fresh catch… and then it's beer chasers on him, with sake and sushi that melt in your mouth. The stall is modest in size and sparsely furnished, but it is packed to the seams with double lines outside straining to get in… We eat as if we are all named Crusoe... and we have still two or more meals to go that day! ■ I do love Tea, especially at precisely 4.00pm where it can be taken in the garden, located on the 41st Floor atrium, in the peaceful Peak Lounge; its serenity complemented by a cluster of beautiful bamboo trees, specially transplanted from Hawaii. It is here that I find myself chatting and sharing publicity, anecdotes, jokes and ideas with Mr. Thompson. The more I visit this most welcoming of hotels, the more I realize that despite the elitism, it retains a marvelous sense of humility and devotion to its international clientele …Tea continues... with the *"we're just here to please"* service…and of course we also have that stunning view of Fuji… ■ I am driving away from The Hyatt-Tokyo this evening to a thunderclap of anger from the skies… perhaps a sign of disapproval from Tokyo's gods … that by daring to leave, I am acting with ingratitude.

JUST DESSERTS-PARIS

I have been to Paris many times...none that romantic, despite being the impossible romantic. I always looked for romantic scenarios but somehow, something never seemed to gel, probably usually due to staying at so-so hotels... ■ The plane touches down at the smaller, more personal airport, that is Orly...definitely something romantic about these smaller airports...I recall "Casablanca"... the fog, like a cotton blanket slowly falling... shades of Rick, slightly misty-eyed as *she* walks away onto an idling aircraft and out of his life...perhaps... *"Paris...we'll always have Paris"*...The taxi drivers are very cheerful. It's after lunch, so they should be...The drive is comfortable and already I feel I am a *Parisian*. ■ Le Park Hyatt Vendome in the Rue de La Paix is a wonder...On the sight of a former bank, there is style and grace as befits a property in the prestigious neighborhood of Place de Vendome ...I sense the affluence and note the proximity of Chanel, Ricci, Gucci, Hermes even Dunhill, next door. This isn't just fashion *ville*...I love wearing black, and lo and behold, as the door is opened at our arrival smart handsome bellboys and concierges appear as a team. *Allez les Bleus* or is it *Noirs?* The cases, all nine of them, are whisked up to our rooms. We are then ushered through the bright and spacious corridor. I note with professional interest, the beautiful conservatory that serves as the public meeting place, with the offset lounges, as well as a coffee shop and breakfast and lunchroom. I spy what appears to be a real fire place, where people are taking their after-lunch coffees and cigars...Ah, the French...I so love their saner attitudes towards political correctness... I feel I belong, so welcome is the greeting, and sincerity, laying waste to the theory that the French are rude... not here, not in this town, not so far...In fact we are treated like returning *Napoleons*...conquering heroes, who will be feted, lauded, pampered, indulged, spoiled, fed to bursting point with delicious foie gras! All of this and lashings of outstanding service...the Park Hyatt syndrome is clearly once more at work! ■ I like the fact that art and *gastronomie* are symbiotic... Food is part of the modern artists' palette and this hotel is one of its brightest colors... Cool, hip, offbeat but dignified and elegant... the style of Versace and the earthiness of Picasso... *"plus fort mes amis!"* The contemporaries have left their artistic signatures... Roseline Granet the sculptor (check her door handles and lighting!) Christiane Durand, Sideo Fromboluti and in the dining rooms, Jaune de Chrome, china by Christian Le Page...Hints of Art Deco eclecticism combine easily with Contemporary...a bow to the East, to India's Grand Master Viswanadhan, whose highly evocative abstracts adorn the Park Dining room – an epicurean theatre of the not-so-absurd with original culinary pieces from brilliant precocious Christian David...I am expected for dinner later that week...so my expectations rise, as I view the theatre kitchen, with open wood-burning grill and a beautiful high-rise, glass-encased wine cellar,

carrying the exceptional to the exquisite. ■ My room is *soooh cool* at this hotel and its design team has created an interesting way to perform one's daily ablutions...I muse...A one-stop bathroom in solid ivory granite... a shower a bath ... the shower cascades from a point in the ceiling and the experience is one of luxury, as you unhurriedly unwind and soak up the steam, bathing in warmth amid light from the very Deco sconces... ■ I look down into the courtyard... I see tranquility, and in my mind, I anticipate my stroll in les Tuilleries and around Sacre Coeur early in the morning ... stopping by at Place du Theatre, a cobbled Montmartre square...the sweet baking aromas of fresh croissant and the roasted flavors of strong black coffee, seducing my senses. Although the waiter is brusque, he is not rude and he smiles after I have ordered, but then he clearly is very happy to chat with the day's first customer...I see the Bateaux Mouches, slowly gliding along the Seine, like graceful swans, despite the crowds of people on the upper decks, the lower deck, containing the adventurous diner who wants his cake and to eat it too - catching the sights of Paris, in this sultry Summer time, whilst imbibing a Macon Villages with his steak - frites... *"bon appetit! Monsieur."* ■ Suddenly I snap out of my daydream! Oh yes...Fauchon...I must to this grand magasin - the shrine of all things gourmet to partake in Marrons Glacées, a promised gift, for my Chanteuse from Toulouse...and for me, Perigourd Truffle...L'escargots...pralines...confiture de pruines...Foie Gras ... St André and a host of wonderful cheeses as only France can produce...and a bottle of Rémy 1738 Accord Royal, surely the MacEnroe of all

cognacs...brilliant, provocative and inspirational...a drink for all seasons... One Hundred and Fifty Euros lighter and I am back with goodies ...the concierge, fluent in several languages, rushes out and grabs them...Free of my burden, I can relax in the ever-popular lounge and gaze out at the secluded terrace, over my iced frappé... ■ Paris, despite these difficult times, seems carefree and kind...I see children and teenagers and older people out, enjoying the weather and the sights and sounds, that make this metropolis delightfully romantic and so unique...the Hotel's appeal, clearly has much to do with my bonhomie and altruistic observations...but then, luxury can make this curmudgeon more than a shade optimistic! ■ I am sorry to have missed Msr. Denise, as he clearly has left word to ensure our continuing comfort and joy. It is *les vacances*, which means that like all good Frenchmen, he's in the heart of France somewhere, enjoying his solitude...But his influence is well conveyed by a staff that always see it your way...Nothing is too difficult for...Is it my imagination?...but aren't the ladies at the front desk like St. Laurent models? Such is their stunning appearance! ■ I have returned after an exceptional evening at Le Meurice, just around the corner, where I have come face to face with a near-perfect performance by a formidable young Master Chef Yannick Alenno, who asks me to convey his best wishes to his youthful contemporary Chef David, knowing that I will be supping there later in the week...Le Meurice is one of the sixties older establishments with a bartender of impeccable credentials - indeed his Kir Royale has to be the world's best, served with a wink a nod and great mirth, much belying his formal approach...one of the City's living legends and leaving me in no doubt, that this encounter has to be a significantly historic episode in my Epicurean Voyage. ■ I linger pensively over one final night cap in this stylish lounge, savoring the atmosphere, while people-watching...the fire burns gently in the grate, reminding me of my family, drinking port and nibbling petit fours, after a long indulgent dinner at my mum's house ...I continue to gaze, imagining my next few days in this eternally Romantic city...I feel the cherubs at work... ■ Patrick from Cognac is downstairs, and over a sparse but delicious breakfast of light whole-wheat toast, fresh black figs and strong French coffee, we discuss the day's events...lunch at George Cinq, followed by dinner here, in the studied elegance of the Neo-Classic, Le Park. I have already been introduced to Chef David...He is a goliath of a man in both stature (a build like a Rugby full back and height of a Michael Jordan) and in his creative skills, with a smile as wide as the Mississippi. Ladies he is handsome... and dashing...and taken - sorry! And he is the talk of Paris, with wonderful displays of cooking ... play it simple - play it complex - no matter how intricate or how easy a dish... he is the man! ■ We arrive, a party of five, for dinner and he is so accommodating, even approaching the table to take the wine order and, although we will be pairing cognacs, I love champagne and it duly arrives...I am alive in Paris and about to indulge in some remarkable...legendary cooking...my pursuit of perfect plates is hotting up...Eat your televisible heart out Graham Kerr...this boy is a gourmet Nijinsky, and he's hot to trot! And the most endearing quality is that he still effortlessly keeps his feet on the ground, with his huge heart and humility and humor...I feel honored to meet him and to share his love for good food. And do try his wood-burning oven - grilled steak - it will knock you for six! (Cricket term, meaning the highest number of runs achieved from single strike of the bat -six runs.) ■ The dinner over, it is late and I join David in the bar with a couple of his staff, we drink some more champagne, whilst discussing the high spots of his stellar haute cuisine. He is up for a Michelin award. He is guaranteed one. I think, as do his contemporaries, it will be two and first time around as well. *Bravo!* ■ The days seem to have flashed by, but we have crammed in a lot...A trip to Cognac to relax at the Rémy Martin headquarters and enjoy a tour of the sprawling estate, drinking Louis XIII from the barrel and indulging in a very satisfying lunch prepared at the Rémy Club by invitation only - we are privileged indeed! The last night...and I find myself strolling; the Champs Elysée, see the girls pass by, some flirt, others entwined in lovers' arms, the cafes are full, as the crowd-watchers have taken over...but people don't stare, they just glance nonchalantly, mainly soaking in the atmosphere of this human tide, as it wanders and meanders, under the bright lights, the Tour d'Eiffel – all Gallic magnificence and grandeur...The Arc de Triomphe...despite its brilliant light...it stands alone...an island...remote, capturing the heart and strength of this idiosyncratic city, while the soul of France's unnamed hero rests...Just a man, with a passion, and a feeling of pride...The French are just the same...No one more so than the Parisian..."*A bientot mes amis!*" ■ So here I am, on a plane heading back to the USA...I have allowed my memories to take root on this Epicurean odyssey...embarking on culinary journeys across the globe...meeting beautiful souls and inspired geniuses, all hand in hand, embroidering and weaving the very substance of this rich tapestry we call life...and food... glorious food...people...places...pabulum...those faraway places with strange-sounding names of which I write, and remember with great fondness...my albeit too-short stays in some magnificent properties, where I discovered a genuine caring, warmth and hospitality, and people who are the unsung heroes, these special people, who with their golden touch make us ordinary mortals feel like Kings, pampering, cosseting and indulging us, so that just for a short period in our lives, we can assume all the trappings of living and enjoying...
the high life!

THE QUALITY O
INVERSE PROPOR
ALTITUDE OF THE
WITH AIRPLANES
EXAMPLE.

FOOD IS IN
ION TO THE
INING ROOM,
HE EXTREME

BRYAN MILLER,
NEW YORK TIMES
FOOD CRITIC

THE FLIGHT OF THE INSATIABLE EPICUREAN

BY DAVID SHAW

I am in an indulgently whimsical state of mind… just thinking. ■ If someone had asked me back in my murky past if I woul[d] like to go around the Far East in 10 days, I would have retorte[d] *"I'm not Phineas Fogg and I do not like balloons…"* o[r] something to that effect… ■ There are many ways o[f] traveling to the Pan-Asian belt these days and certainly by air [is] the best way… and as my itinerary was to begin in Sydne[y] followed by Singapore, Hong Kong and Tokyo, I felt that th[e] tried and trusted airline …Queensland and Northern Territori[es] Air Services had the experience, the service the quality and th[e] comfort to ensure an easy passage as I embarked on m[y] epicurean odyssey… ■ Sometimes I never cease to amaz[e] myself and have to pinch various parts of my anatomy t[o] convince myself of the reality of good situations… so here I a[m] sitting in the first class section of an airline that pursue[s] excellence in every part of its worldwide `operation. It is ve[ry] hard not to appreciate the sunny optimism and generosity th[at] exists in the habitants from *"Down Under."* ■ The spirit of Oz is alive and well, and the beaming smile, as wide as the Oz outbac[k] is omnipresent… *"Glass of bubbly, sir before we depart, or was it two…?"*-97 Charles Heidsieck… mmm…not a bad house. Glancing round, I notice the obvious appreciation of the other passengers … the young couple gazing into each other's eyes, fo[r] them perhaps a journey on their journey of life full of good things maybe a bit of turbulence…but always flying high in their hope[s] and dreams…interesting parallels-*"n'est ce pas?"* On the aisle seat down the front I observe a man huddles over his laptop… th[e] glasses piling up, as he thrashes away on the keyboard at the speed of a "Roadrunner" … should he worry? *"No worries, mate, w[e] will get you there and in the most work conducive circumstances, if it's essentially work you need to do, on our watch… We'll eve[n] have an ad hoc in-flight help yourself service available if you don't want to wait for our set mealtimes…"* I notice other busine[ss] types and despite their hardened sophistication to airline travel, they appear just as thrilled to be here as I am and the other relativ[e] naifs! As for me well I am supposed to be working, but I am one of the luckier ones, I write about food and travel… a bon vivar[t] if ever there was one and I get to enjoy all of this overwhelming hospitality and cosseting, where nothing is too much trouble. ■ I am magnetized by ergonomically-designed cutting-edge contraptions…ah the marvels of modern travel its seems that ever[y] airline worth its salt is hell bent on pioneering the perfect flat bed /armchair. These guys seem to have got it right after watchin[g] their peers try a plethora of combinations, before deciding and investing in their final choice. But here indeed I am lounging i[n] the new and innovative "Sky-bed", designed by leading Aussie Marc Newson it is a work of art… ■ Consider this… a booth wit[h] a sliding partition, in case you are not well acquainted with your next door neighbor… think all leather sumptuous luxurious .[..] think loads of space … you definitely could swing a cat in here… think a working and dining area that will accommodate a thre[e]

In pursuit of the perfect plate… Aiming high with friendly spirits and in excellent spirits with the Spirit of Australia

course meal, your laptop plugged in of course, a glass or two of wine and your Oxford English Dictionary and Collins Encyclopaedia of Quotes (both 500 pages thick) and a copy of one's essential reading…the London Sunday Times (with its eight sections!), an armchair controlled by the press of the in-built control fascia, resembling the moon shuttle, a bendy reading spot-light… a TV set with a gazillion channels, and a flat bed that guarantees you sleep the entire way… and you have the shape and future of things to come by this antipodean airline's investment in customer safety, comfort, care and service… I can sleep, I can work I can socialize, I can indulge, I can collapse into a potato couch… I can channel surf … I can adapt a myriad roles in my journey… ■ I have traveled with the best in my insatiable quest for the perfect plate…India Egypt Taiwan Germany South Africa, Japan, Hong Kong,

England France Switzerland, Greece Spain Italy Portugal... but nowhere have I flown in such comfort luxury and above all personal convenience... it pleases me to be able please myself...And all thanks to my benevolent and ultra-efficient hosts in the sky... ■ *Not only in the Spirit of Excellence but also in the Spirit of Friendship...*

My Far-eastern Epicurean Extravaganza begins...

I first flew in an airplane some 39 years ago at the tender age of eighteen years. It was on a Boeing 707 and I must have taken off and landed at least 10 times en route from London to Madras, India. I was excited... I was scared... I was optimistic... I was in love... I was depressed... (I was in a tentative courtship of Kay-she subsequently four years later became the first Mrs. Shaw-but she was also still keen on Fred... her most recent boyfriend... and he was returning to London... after two weeks in Germany with his Mum and Dad... And I was off for 8 weeks... Eight weeks!!! That long-a lifetime-Dear God!-Would she still love me...Out of sight out of mind...) Then there was my idiot older brother (he's not really-but he seemed idiotic at the time!) sitting next to me, making planes –in-distress noises, with a high pitched whine, as I clutched my little photo of my loved one even tighter!!! You get the picture, first flight nerves and all that! ■ Things have changed since then of course, I am not scared, I am not so depressed, though I am still in love (I am pursuing closure on the potential of Mrs. Shaw the third!) But, unlike Jean's comments, and the scaremongers that have suddenly found voice since the recent turbulent times, flying today, especially in Business and First Class and especially with international carriers such as this is a gas!

A Change for Good and in One World...

I am privileged and thrilled to be flying with this airline for one other reason. It has adopted the wonderful humane cause UNICEF and on every flight, one can hear the appeal from Roger Moore (the former and very suave James Bond and now Sir Roger) Not surprisingly with his devoted and indefatigable service for this most noble of humane cause, and in his capacity as International Goodwill Ambassador for UNICEF, having been passed the torch by Audrey Hepburn, his original mentor, Roger has raised several millions of pounds through Qantas and its partner One World airlines including Singapore Cathay Pacific and British Airways amongst others. As we approach the descent we are advised that there are packets in the seat-backs for any donations of foreign notes and coins that will speedily find their way into the UNICEF funds to stem the horrific flow of 28,000 kids dying a day. A sobering thought but a necessary one when all around me I observe anything but suffering and hardship...

Getting into the Spirit...

Their new face these days is John Travolta. He purchased an old Boeing from them for his own personal use. (He is qualified to fly jumbos-believe it or not!) He, by chance, stopped by in Sydney to have it serviced by Qantas. Whilst there, he made friends with the Chairman and as a result a friendship was forged and he has now become the airline's official voice-which should drive most red-blooded ladies into a Saturday Night fever! ■ Mr. Magoo aka my colleague (thank God his name isn't Jones!) and I arrive at LAX in a state of great expectation, we like the look of the desk crew, they seemed to have been blessed with smiles as friendly as the Aussie sun. Checking in is easy despite the five cases we have lugged in! After some publicity shots in the cabin (security cleared` of course and stringently so-naturally!) it now that we are found, sipping our Charles Heidsieck 1997 and enjoying some Neil Perry-inspired hors d'oeuvres in their well stocked and well-appointed hospitality lounge...waiting for our flight to be called! ■ Half the fun of traveling First Class these days with these sunny people from "the land from down under" is the preceding expectancy, as much as actually doing it. It is one sublime experience with surprise and delight following like a David Copperfield-unraveling of incomprehensible trick after trick... So it comes as no surprise to report, based on considerable personal experience, that they are easily within the top five operators today. Easily! Even my very cynical associate glancing at my scribble, mumbles his approval through his Neil Perry canapé of goose terrine and glass of bubbly! ■ The leather armchair seating folds flat into a really nice chaise allowing supreme comfort for such a long journey (13 ½ hours!) and of course the

"I feel about airplanes the way I feel about diets. It seems to me that they are wonderful things for other people to go on."-Jean Kerr (Modern US Dramatist)

state-of-the-art hi-tech at your fingertips, is not a maze of buttons and slides that has you leveling and rearranging the posture of yourself and the person immediately behind you! And nor do you have to attend an astronaut's training course to follow the instructions. *"Keep it simple mate!"*-A wonderfully traditional Aussie philosophy. ■ The age of travel is no way better illustrated than by this crew. For a start they have an extraordinarily dapper in-flight Managing Director. Dapper in a navy blue chalk-stripe suit, with carnation in button-hole (should have been a wattle, guys!-but still, carnation is good) and most helpful, he is an obliging host as he makes suggestions for our opening meal.

Sugar and Spice and all things nice...

And of course you can expect the finest food as their World Class chef and mate of mine-Neil Perry from Sydney, works his culinary magic to bring fliers, his dazzling array of specialties, including Chicken with a Pumpkin Seed Sauce and Mango Salsa and fragrant rice, or a tender flaky Salmon Fillet with Roast Vegetables asparagus and mushroom sauce, or a Salad of Beef with braised capsicum and pesto. For you vegetarians he also offers an Italian Tomato and Herb soup, Eggplant Parmigiana with basil oil, Green Leaf Salad with red wine vinaigrette. So much for the sit down stuff... if you want to go casual and just graze when you feel like it...wandering down the galley you discover a sumptuous buffet laid out with wondrous dishes and treats... even enjoy a delectable Toasted Pastrami, Rocket and Mustard Baguette... a delish Carrot and Honey Soup, fresh whole fruit... figs... kiwis... mango... ■ Fancy a slap up breakfast when they gently wake you... sun streaming through the window refracts through the glasses of fresh juices and on to the gleaming cutlery... the *"Berry Energizer"* becomes an

instant hit *"an energizing dairy based health drink with honey fresh fruit and yogurt..."* so the description goes. Scrambled egg... toast roast vine tomatoes portobellos... smoked salmon... sausages... bacon.... Ah the sizzle and the aromas...Enough!!! I've only brought three suits with me... still the tailor in Hong Kong awaits me tape-measure-bedecked neck, ready to make the necessary alterations! ■ *"I am wary of confusing the concept of fusion, so that we do not end up with Con-fusion! I am different, in that I stay main-frame on the type of dishes I offer; not just Thai or French inspired but Indian, Italian-all having their original bases. Which is how Oz cooking has evolved. Don't think Pacific-Rim and all that bollocks! This is different, because we offer regional cooking which underlines our Oz identity. So it is very much the same as the fabric of the Aussie or Sydney social make up. This is a city that socially has recognized that the various ethnic fabrics create a rich common tapestry that works economically and socially in the city and the country. Sydnians have an identity of their own. Just as New York has been inspired by its multi-ethnicity so has Sydney. But whereas restaurants in NY are definitively French, Italian or Contemporary American, we have the typically Aussie restaurant blending the best of these cultural identities into the cooking!"-Neil Perry-Rockpool Restaurant (Sydney)* ■ Very much the enfant terrible of the Aussie dining scene and making sure that Sydney-has taken up the challenge for the title of the food capital of Australia, Neil Perry is to be also congratulated for three things: his success of the Rockwell, his strong relationship with this international airline as their food designer and consultant, and the brilliant meals in First and Business Class. ■ *" I met all these Qantas bigwigs at an International convention at the Hilton in 1960 something, and they invited me onto the selection panel, because I was supposedly the "blue eyed boy" for the marketing of table wines. Since 1964, I've been there, selecting their wines for*

them. In 1967 they made me chairman of the panel. This was honorary. But then we were gainfully employed from 1968 onwards. There were only two other consultants in the 80s. They then increased this to five. The regular panel includes John Hanley, Ian Mackenzie, and various other wine celebs. The whole system is one of, we ask for tenders and offers. We get literally hundreds and then we put these into the line up under categories and we do not know the makes just the rows of glasses for the tasting. Like any other wine exposition, we taste determine and select. It is easier because we can discard the ones that clearly are not going to happen. We then judge the next tier. We then select a final pool of 10, from which we will select 4 or 5. We of course have to be careful with the delicate older wines. I am not one to worry about altitude. Champagne at 30,000 feet is the perfect environment for me. But Qantas have done a

fabulous job in promoting the Oz wine industry. And perhaps we should all be grateful for that. They have been at the forefront in flying the flag. Qantas is also getting into offering the best upper echelon wine, by getting smaller lots and grater variety. It is wonderful to see that everyone is encouraged to present their wines to Qantas, which is no longer the province of the big boys. And of course the food, courtesy of Neil Perry adds to their top-notch service"-Len Evans OBE. ■ Australian Dining and Wining (not whining that is us Pommies' domain!) has emerged over recent years to take its now rightful stage in world Cuisine. People like Perry and his good friend the great Tetsuya are exemplary cooks. They also enjoy the added advantage of being able to pair their creations with the world class wines that Australian wineries such as Penfold's, Banrock Wynn's, Lindeman's Hardy's, Wolf Blass et al, have to offer. Choice is great and variety wondrous. Qantas, thanks to their perceptive selection of Len Evans, OBE, one of the founding fathers of the Australian Wine Industry, as their very own Wine Consultant, has been able to create the perfect pairing 25,000 feet up. Classic Semilion, Riesling Chardonnay, Shiraz and Cabernets all had their day, being enjoyed by two receptive palates throughout this delightful aeronautical extravaganza. ■ Then it is time for coffee with a Cointreau, petit fours, and some cheese from a groaning cheese board and it's "Let's go to the Movies" which includes The Italian Job , Anger Management and a host of light entertainment shows, or simply a glance or two at their in-flight Magazine (complete with Mr. Travolta on the cover!) which puts most retail publications to shame by its sheer entertainment and editorial content...

ZZZ...

As snug as bugs in a rug, all around me fellow travelers are in bed-adjusting mode... a cushion here, a sleep suit there and soon all are drifting into a sound sleep, later to be gently stirred by a cheery crewmember with hot towels and a refreshing cup of "rosie" (Rosy Lee-tea. Rhyming slang!) And then the serious focus on the aforementioned gargantuan breakfast, which also I should mention includes as an option a Baked Egg with Roast Capsicum and Zucchini, Vine-ripened Tomato and Bacon. But for me it has to be the addictive "Berry Energiser" genuinely good fortifying stuff and certainly the breakfast of this ersatz champion! ■ We approach a dawning Sydney... I can envisage a busy George Street making ready for the day's inner city life...it is about this time that the first ferry is chugging out to Bondai Beach riding along on a crest of the waves... I hear the morning call of the Kookaburra... The Saturday Street market is stirring into tent enshrouded life as the cheery stall holders busy themselves... awaiting the first early-morning browser in search of the arts and crafts of local artists, down by the Rocks... "Australia, Australia... we love ya!" ■ But all good things must come to an end and so with the final approach into Sydney, and our expectations once more aroused, we land as gracefully as a dove in flight, hugely enthused and impressed by this trademark Spirit of Friendship that is so unmistakably Australian.

...Game on!

P
A
N

ASIAN

P
R
O
M
I
S
E

SPIRIT OF OZ

Chocolate Assiette paired with Rémy Martin V.S.O.P

See me... feel me, ■ *Touch me... feel me,* ■ *...Listening to you, I get the music. Following you, I feel the beat Right behind you, I see the glory. I get excited at your feet."* ■ *Tommy- a Rock Opera by Peter Townsend.* ■ The plaintive voice of the "deaf, dumb and blind kid" Tommy pierces through the apathy of a post - war Britain, in the retro 50's. In as much the same way, the striking notes and dramatic overtones of Aria has shaken the dining foundations of Sydney. Aria is a freedom movement to a release of the senses. Inspirational, controversial, profound and clearly with a message is

Crisp Chinese Skin Barramundi, shaved abalone, choy sun, prawn dumpling

paired with Rémy Martin V.S.O.P

the celebrated cuisine of Chef Matt Moran who together with longtime friend confidante and partner, Peter Sullivan, presents an uncompromising menu of Contemporary Australian cuisine. ■ Moran is an embodiment of the spirit of Sydney's Culinary ascendancy onto the world stage and just as surely as the genius of Who's leader Pete Townsend, he has rocked the establishment with his home grown talents. The setting for his subliminal chords of presentation balance and taste is a spectacular vista of the Opera House, just a few bars away across the quayside. ■ Moran's intriguing starters are a compelling recitative with items such as a Soy Marinated Tuna served with a salad of mint peanuts and red curry dressing; and Baked Swiss brown Mushrooms with hommus eggplant and salsa verde that will have you in ecstasy. ■ Continuing this passionate aria are entrees of exceptional note...Confit of Bangalow Pork Belly

with Cumquat Jam and baby leaf salad and the signature Five Spiced Quail Breast with Peking Duck and sweet and sour cherries, certainly in both instances, a case of *"if food be the music of love"!* ■ And as if in final reprise of good taste, the dining experience has to end unequivocally on a high note with Chef Moran's quite strident dessert menu, where the textures of a Chocolate Assiette, consisting of an arrangement of Valrhona chocolate delicacies, beat out a tasteful staccato rhythm that simply floods the senses!

Confit of Bangalow Pork Belly, sea scallops and cumquat jam

paired with Rémy Martin XO Excellence

Grilled Scampi & Barramundi On Trompettes de la Mort, Zucchini, Thyme paired with Rémy Martin V.S.O.P iced

Moscovado Sugar & Macadamia Semifreddo with Poached Bosc Pear paired with Rémy Martin XO Excellence

"Ah... get yourself a chair Katie... and pull up one for me... and fix the drinks". Humphrey Bogart (winding up Katherine Hepburn on The African Queen set, after she had nagged him and John Huston about the perils of drink. ■ A nonsequitor? True! But this particular quote reminds us of the great star quality that was once enjoyed by Hollywood where the true stars could act and exuded a degree of both humor and humility... ■ Much the same is true about Peter Doyle (his culinary feats at the late departed Celsius are legendary). ■ With the perfect backdrop of the stylish soaring loft that is Est, where the tables are elegantly dressed with sparkling flatware and napery, and the odd artifacts abound, Doyle is a man who has never ceased to smile at himself and is mindful of the slender line between stardom and ignominy. ■ Like a phoenix rising he has created Est establishing this

Chef Peter Doyle

Rillettes of Duck

paired with Rémy Martin V.S.O.P

downtown nightspot into the hottest dining room in New south Wales. ■ The results whilst bordering on the spectacular are nevertheless not unexpected such is the quality and touch of Chef Doyle's work. A towering presentation of Grilled Scampi with Barramundi demonstrates flavor and harmony and texture... The Rilletes of Duck, seared and served rare are approaching the sublime and the Breast of Squab served with morelles, cabbage and broad beans is both a study in flavor and presentation. ■ And then it's back to the not unenviable procedure of serious eating with an array of... sweet sensations including a hugely enjoyable Moscavado, Sugar and Macadamia Semi-freddo...Umm...I glance around this sophisticated dining room, noticing the eager Saturday night crowds and the wait for a table... aah... lucky me!

GALILEO

SYDNEY

"If you want a place in the sun, expect to get a few blisters" - Loretta Young (on the price of stardom) ■ With a blend of Japanese design and symmetry and the classic foundations of France, Executive Chef Harunobu Inukai is the compelling reason why the Observatory's Galileo is enjoying a meteoric renaissance. It doesn't get much better than this! Dining in a one of the quite brilliant Orient - Express properties' top - drawer, internationally acclaimed 5-star restaurant is pure euphoria! ■ I savored these observations, sitting in the yesteryear surroundings of the Galileo -

Galileo ■ Chef Harunobu Inukai

absorbing the richness of the fine tapestries, exquisite walnut furniture, unusual artifacts and objets d'art, the correctness of the elegantly attired wait-staff and the hushed reverent atmosphere . . . ■ Newcomer, Chef Inukai has quickly settled. Chosen for his great verve and passion for world cuisine and his international experience, including Paris, he has more than rekindled Galileo's magnificent reputation... ■ The menu now easily satisfies the most critical of pundits with stellar items that cause much procrastination! But the wait-staff is patient and quite

indulgent... after much thought, we gave in to the opening gambits of a Trio of Pressed Duck - served as Duck Confit, Breast and Foie Gras, presented with Savoy cabbage Honey dressing... and the Pizza Tart (memories perhaps of Chef Inukai's sojourns in France where a local favorite is the very similar pissaladiere,) captures the senses in an instant, the potato and beetroot working in tandem with the onion comfit and truffle. ■ The main courses reflect, with some panache, Mr. Inukai's accomplished skills and his regional French influences combined with his native Japan: Roasted Venison, delicately layered with Spiced Apple and

Foie Gras salad, Beluga lentils and Sauce Poivrade... and a Roulade of Squab, ingeniously treated with Scallops shiitake Mushrooms and Barley and chicken Jus... the myriad textures had our taste buds orbiting faster than Haley's Comet! ■ With two forks and the piece de resistance of Chocolate Fondant and Pistachio Ice-cream with our chilled Remy VSOP and we had reached seventh heaven... and the impression that the Galileo truly is a restaurant fit for the stars!

Roulade of Squab

paired with Rémy Martin XO Excellence

Chocolate Fondant

paired with Rémy Martin Extra

Roasted Venison
paired with Rémy Martin V.S.O.P

Duck Confit, Breast & Foie Gras

paired with Rémy Martin Extra

Grilled
Ocean
Trout

paired with
Rémy Martin
XO Excellence
iced

What is it about the Park Hyatt Group. Is it its chic and sleek approach to hospitality? Or is it an uncompromising desire to simply be the best? And perhaps that is the key - Simplicity. Thus it should come as no surprise to our regular readers to find that here I was yet once more discovering a superb restaurant within a Park Hyatt property. I have enjoyed the stellar cuisine at the New York Grill and Bar at the Park Hyatt in Tokyo, I have tasted the whimsical creativity of Sandro Gamba at NoMI in Chicago's Park Hyatt, and here I was , in Sydney, enjoying the enterprising talents of one of the city's most accomplished chefs Anthony Musarra! ■ And can this Oz cook, *"fair dinkum"!* ■ The fact of the matter is that this chef has an uncluttered, unpretentious approach to his craft. His presentation is pure modern cuisine technique, based on using the pick of indigenous ingredients. The result? An award -winning menu, offering the Epicurean, a choice of innovative, classics with

Coconut
Panacotta

paired with
Rémy Martin
V.S.O.P

Chef Anthony Musarra

Lamb
Saltimbocca

paired with
Rémy Martin
XO Excellence

just a hint of influence from the Mediterranean region. ■ The interior, designed by Tony Chi, provides a complementing back ground to this *"wizard from Oz"*. Minimalist, yet stylish, and with a breathtaking view of the Opera House, it was so easy to sit and be indulged at the candlelit table, embracing that wonderful Sydney atmosphere. ■ And oh what wondrous tastes Duck Rillettes with toasted sourdough, roasted pear cornichons and spring onion; or the Wood Roasted Barramundi with fennel, confit potato gratin and red wine. And the so very unique textures of the Grilled Terrine of White Rabbit, sage and pinenut gnocchi, black cabbage and sherry reduction. ■ With chefs of Musarra's caliber, it is small wonder that Sydney with its God - given climate, fresh produce, natural resources, and the sunniest of people, has finally emerged to take the world culinary stage by storm. ■ *Good on yer mate!*

HARBOUR
KITCHEN

SYDNEY

ROCKPOOL

SYDNEY

Salad of Mud Crab and Crispy Pork Belly with Som Dtam

paired with Rémy Martin V.S.O.P iced

Fillet of Barramundi poached in Coconut Milk with Garam Masala

paired with Rémy Martin V.S.O.P on the rocks

Rockpool
■ **Chef Neil Perry**

"Let's hope that in the future we will all be able to enjoy tuna sashimi, salt and pepper squid, lobster salad, grilled John Dory, and even the humble fish and chips...Don't we owe our children that much" ■ Neil Perry is very much the chef of the moment in his homeland of Oz. Not for a second complacent with his successful TV series, Foodsource, and blessed with more than a soupcon of environmental awareness...hence the comment in support of the Marine Stewardship Council (MSC) which is a partnership set up by World Wildlife Fund and Unilever to prevent overfishing especially with some endangered species ■ *"Rockpool is a culmination of all the things that have influenced my career and my life...and is a reflection of my experiences and thoughts on cooking... "*
■ It is humid outside on a bustling hot August night, but inside all is as serene and calm as the ocean...still waters run deep as we are offered a myriad dishes of all things seafood, but of course for some of us carnivores, there are other Perry delicacies... ■ In a menu of spectacular flair and dimension, we enjoy diverse tastes and savor sheer culinary conjuring...Fresh from the Sea affords us to indulge in Salad of Mud Crab and Crispy Pork Belly with a sensory startling accompaniment of Cashew Nut Nam Jim and Som Dtom... And before our excitement has barely subsided... a wonderfully structured dish... Hapuka cooked in a Pot with Garam Masala and Coconut Milk which is served with Semolina Noodles and Snowpeas...shades of the Esplanade, way back in the 50's in Singapore ■ But I am nothing if indulgent especially when it comes to affairs of the stomach...my eyes lock onto a particularly intriguing item. This time a Perry signature – the Chinese Roast Pigeon with Prawn - stuffed eggplant, stir fried Chinese broccoli and black vinegar sauce... the explosion of flavors reminiscent of a fire works display on July 4th ...
■ A quick moment to reposition and savor the earlier highlights and then it's Strawberries and Cream – Perry's Desserts. In this instance an unforgettable Caramel Mousse with White chocolate sauce Coffee hazelnuts and Cumquats...indeed I only have eyes for you!

Caramel Mousse with White Chocolate sauce, Hazelnuts and Cumquats

paired with Rémy Martin XO Excellence chilled

**Roasted Squab with Buckwheat & Chestnut Mushrooms
paired with Rémy Martin Extra iced**

"Tetsuya is part of an elite group of international chefs, along with Girardet, Ducasse, Boulud, Adria and Keller, that has influenced other chefs through their personal styles and unique approaches to food." – Charlie Trotter

I am back at this landmark restaurant, to meet up with the great man...My charming companion, quite fetching in red Chinese silk and I, inhaling the cool sophisticated atmosphere of this temple to beautiful cooking. A flute of Pol Roger, and we are ready for this sumptuous degustation of 18 courses... ■ An amuse-bouche of Tuna Cocktail with wasabi jelly...and then an auspicious, delicate beginning, with Tasmanian Pacific Oysters with rice vinegar and ginger to accompany our iced VSOP, along with a Chestnut Mushroom Soup, scented with truffle, we have to admire the presentation, cleverly fashioned in the Japanese mould. Again, drawing on his traditions, Tetsuya's Tartare of Tuna with fresh wasabi, forms part of a sextet also consisting of Marinated Fillet of Trevally with preserved lemon, set on sushi rice, a Tataki of Venison with rosemary and honey, and three other delicately presented tastings. ■ A slight pause and we steal time to absorb the omnipresent serenity and the contrasting starkness of black on white exemplifying classic Japanese cubic simplicity. Calm, with a vista of the beautiful tranquil Japanese garden with its limpid pools, creates the ambiance required for the on-going spectacle. ■ And then, with much panache and whimsy by our waiter, it is time to experience the depth of Chef's understanding of fish - a confit of Tasmanian Trout (a Tetsuya original!) together with Ocean Trout Roe and marinated celery-very much an indigenously Australian item. Again, credit to Chef Akuda for his ability to shape and blend. ■ More delectable surprises… this

Tasmanian Pacific Oysters with Rice Wine Vinaigrette

paired with Rémy Martin V.S.O.P chilled

time some masterful Lobster Ravioli, warm Salad of Grilled Cuttlefish Scallop with Foie Gras. And then almost effortlessly, Tetsuya's art shifts into overdrive with a presentation of panache and dazzle… Steamed Murray Cod, Braised Ox Cheek, Roasted Breast of Squab, Rolled Wagyu Beef - *"My goodness-enough!"*- I hear my new designer frock coat screaming…. ■ …so who can truly follow this Grand Wizard's act!

Chocolate Terrine with Cognac Anglaise & Mascarpone Mousse

paired with Rémy Martin XO Excellence chilled

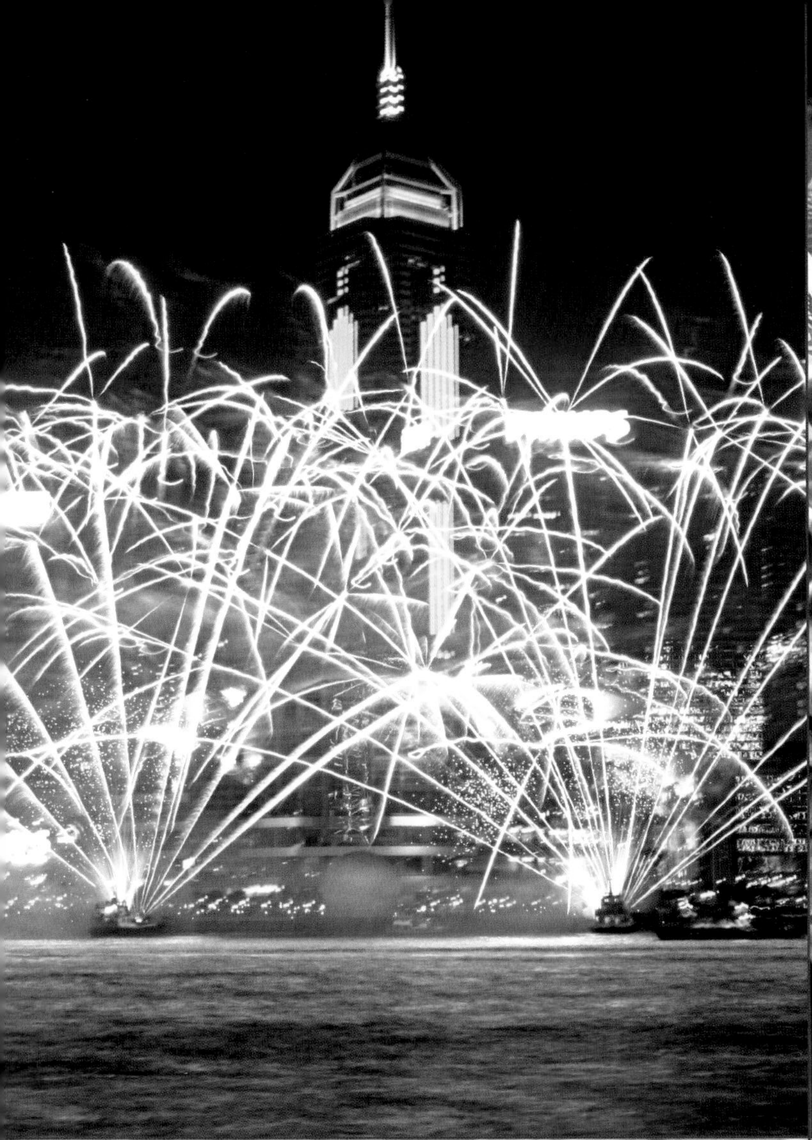

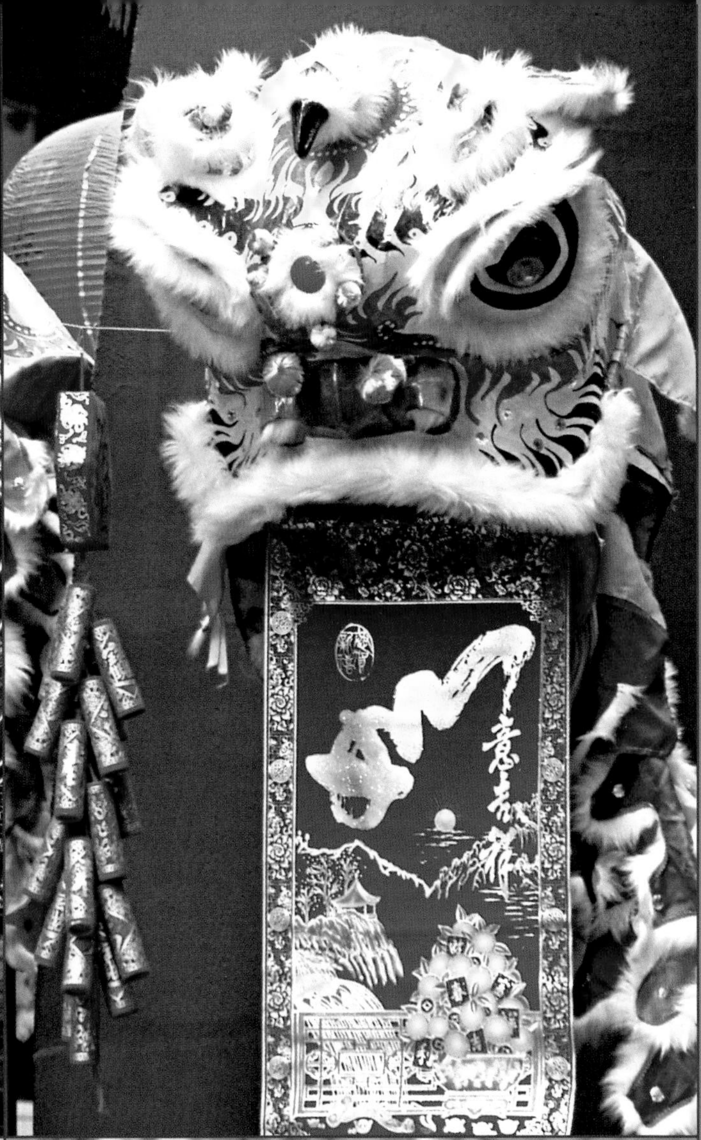

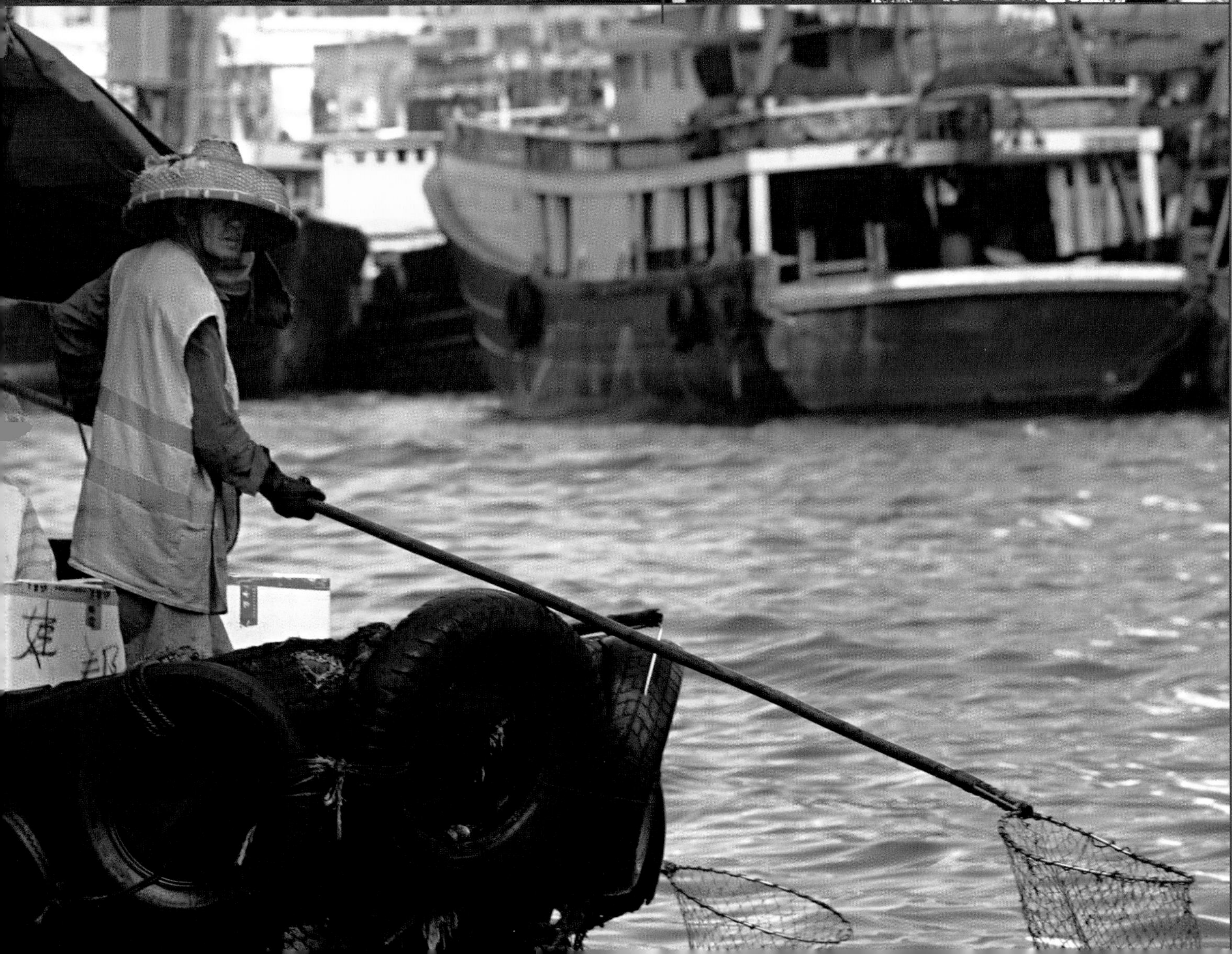

LAND OF THE DRAGON DANCE

GRISSINI

HONG
KONG

"Man cannot live by bread alone" ■ Unless of course it happens to be at Grissini! High-rise Hong Kong's cutting edge architecture provides a spectacular setting for this stylish jewel in the Hyatt empire. ■ If you like the taste and smell of fresh bread then look no further. ■ Grissini is named after the popular Italian bread stick. And as you step into this ultra-chic dining room that dominates this stylish hotel, you will see the wood burning oven from which wafts the to-die-for aromas of its freshly baked bread sticks. ■ Robert Barker, the Grand Hyatt's general manager extraordinaire has recruited a talented chef de cuisine to maintain Grissini's ambitious drive to its world-class stage. All you Californians are familiar with Beverly Hills' Il Ciello, which is where the precocious talents of Chef Vittorio Lucariello emerged. ■ The food is both a delight and full of flavor. In these hi-tech retro opulent surroundings accentuated by splashes of black and chrome, dining here is a memorable experience of an ingenious presentation of classic regional Italian fare. The starters dazzle and captivate... Smoked

**Smoked Sturgeon and Tuna Rolls
with Lemon Caper Couscous
paired with Rémy Martin Extra with water**

**Grilled Scampi on Zucchini purée
paired with Rémy Martin V.S.O.P**

**Grilled Pork Chop on Lemon Sage sauce
paired with Rémy Martin XO Excellence on rocks**

**Neapolitan Eggplant Terrine with
Tomato Confit and Citronella Ice Cream
paired with Rémy Martin Extra lightly chilled**

Sturgeon and Tuna roll with a lemon caper cous - cous, or the more traditional Gratinated Grilled Eggplant rolls, filled with mozzarella in a tomato sauce ... A swift gear change in this Lamborghini of a menu that is all exhilarating power, style and thrills and you are flying with some adrenalin boosting entrees including Grilled Scampi on Zucchini Purée, or a rare Grilled Sea Bream on porcini herb sauce... a spell binding Baked Duck

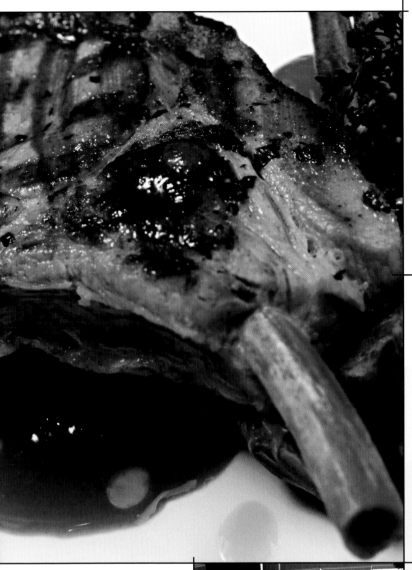

Grissini ■ Chef Vittorio Lucariello

Breast with dried figs and foie gras... no matter what your choice Chef Vittoria is the man! ■ And then even more impossible sensory highs, with the dessert cart... an absolutely daring Neapolitan Eggplant Terrine with tomato confit and citronella Ice cream... *whaaat!* Hot Chocolate Pudding, with hazelnut Ice cream and raspberry sauce... a variation on a theme with the Panna Cotta with Rhubarb Compote and Strawberries...simply presented but with complex textures...In short, this boy can cook! ■ Hong Kong not only welcomes you Chef Vittorio-it embraces you!

INAGIKU
HONG KONG

Inagiku ■ Chef Yumoto Makoto

Caramelized Lobster with Japanese Black Pepper paired with Rémy Martin XO Excellence on the rocks

Below

**Lily Root & Pumpkin
Marble Ball with
Green Tea Cream Sauce**

**paired with
Rémy Martin
V.S.O.P Iced**

The Inagiku family was originally respected the world over for their far- flung empire taking in New York amongst other established "*food*" cities. In recent times and with a changed policy, the family still allows the name to be used, but these days instead of the original traditional décor of a regime ancien, you will find modernism... vibrant colors... shapes... reflecting a fusion of history with voguish décor more befitting Shiseido and Armani than the earlier Shogun Dynastic folklore. ■ One thing though has remained - the synonymy between Inagiku and Tempura. The tempura style of Japanese Cuisine has long been a staple on offer to Inagiku's international clientele. Tempura was derived from the ancient Portuguese explorers of Vasco Digamma's day-"*temporo*"–Portuguese for "*cooking*" with vegetables and fish in a deep fried fashion. ■ Under the stellar control of chef de Cuisine Yumoto Makoto, Inagiku not only offers this but all elements of modern Japanese Cuisine, including Teppanyaki, Sushi and a range of wholesome and exceedingly indulgent desserts. ■ Makoto, loyal to his native Japan, offers a delicacy and artistry in his approach. The result is a presentation that fits like a glove with the

ambience of a stylish restaurant incorporating a harmonious blend of Japanese originality and tradition with a vibrancy of contemporary accents. ■ Pick of the original tempura dishes are an authentic rendition of light Deep-fried Prawns with a Vegetable cake and the altogether impressive Live King Prawn Tempura. With Makoto now in his element we enjoyed the continuing introductory Inagiku degustation with several varieties of his Sashimi and Sushi - all handmade lovingly and artistically for us at the Sushi bar... Ark Shell...Tuna Rolls..Fatty tuna...Oshi Sushi... item by item was like discovering King Solomon's Mines. More innovation from the magic fingers of this clever chef followed with some show-stopping signatures especially of note were the Vinegared Eel and Cucumber, Tuna Fish with taro puree and the beef Sukiyaki. ■ Like some deep philosophy, the food, almost in sympathy with the surrounding Zen elements and the concept of "*Flow*" of the sand gardens and waterfalls at the entrance, literally "*flows*" from preparation to presentation to participation. In a word "*Flowless!*"

Right

**Chilled Egg Custard
with Sea Urchin Shell**

**paired with
Rémy Martin Extra
on the rocks**

"She had that beautiful body and the timeless loveliness of her face …But if she had nothing but her voice, she could break your heart with it" Ernest Hemingway (of Marlene Dietrich) ■ "…I'm falling in love again, Never wanted to, What am I to do? I can't help it…"-Friedrich Hollander (Ufaton –Verlag GMBH) ■ It was an unforgettable evening in a Hong Kong that for me had taken on a most romantic hue. Across a very private table sat the Chanteuse, that sultry mysterious Forties Face beguiling me…How appropriate that Ms. Dietrich's words caught my imagination…how appropriate that I should be in love again after such a long time …and how could I not be in this simply delightful diva of a restaurant…Margaux …so different…so elegant …so very French… ■ Commanding fabulous views of the harbour with an incredible neon high-rise backdrop, Margaux is a Romantic's Paradise…an oasis amidst the bustle of busy Kowloon. ■ Elegant décor suggesting the neo-classicism of the dining room of a grand fin de siecle chateau with contrasting contemporary accents, Margaux embraces lovers …be it for people or food. Indulgent service, and inspiringly soulful cuisine from the talented New Zealander, master chef Christopher Christie assure a divinely memorable evening here. ■ Our sojourn was a manifestation of perfection. Everything worked, from the welcoming flutes of champagne, the beautifully set table with Hong Kong Harbour at its exhilarating best and the delicate amuses bouche… to that last sip of cognac as our eyes met… ■ For her…an array of exotic soups and vegetables…degustation style… very thoughtful I mused…. they had only found out that she was vegetarian, minutes before our arrival. ■ The appetizers were entrancing…set my taste buds dancing, as I savored the Sweet Tuiles, filled with crayfish and ratatouille on a light goats cheese mousse… And then a weakness I must confess… the Pan-fried Duck Liver with an apple mousse and caramelized walnuts… ■ Then two sampler -size entrees for me, both clear indications of this amazing understated ability of a chef who inevitably earns his status as one of the industry's finest exponents of uncompromisingly French haute -cuisine. Both reflected his innovative creativity-Noisettes of Lamb with truffle in a crepinette tomato and tarragon, and a Seared Tuna Steak served with snails and capsicum rolls ginger and spiced oil…Merveilleux! ■ And then desserts that would daunt even Escoffier, including a stand -out Christie house signature- Margaux Shortbread - walnut biscuits and cognac served with fig ice-cream. ■ I can be forgiven for seeing the two now in my mind's eye… Her face also… so very timeless… so very classically French… and of course Margaux… We'll always have Margaux…

MARGAUX

HONG

KONG

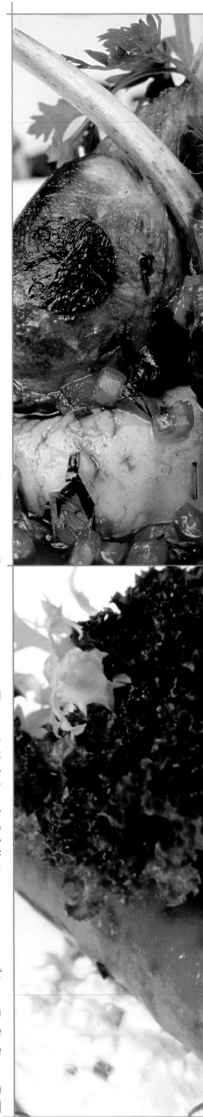

Right

Sweet Tuiles filled with crayfish and ratatouille on goats cheese mousse

paired with Rémy Martin V.S.O.P iced

Left

Noisettes of Lamb

paired with
Rémy Martin
Extra
chilled lightly

Below

Margaux Shortbread with
velour nut biscuits with
cocoa strata & cognac

paired with
Rémy Martin
XO Excellence

Margaux ■
Chef Christopher Christie

ONE HARBOUR ROAD

HONG KONG

Chef Li Shu-Tim

Right

Braised Pork Ribs in "Wu Shek" Style

paired with Rémy Martin Extra

Unpretentious, One Harbour Road reflects a Hong Kong past that was revered for its style and elegance. Chef Li Shu-Tim its executive chef brings that past to life with a fusion of spices shapes and flavors that are the hallmarks of a Cantonese cuisine, big on flavor…big on portions. As he succinctly states, "*No foreign influences no nouvelle nuances-just tradition on my plates lovingly prepared and graciously presented*". ■ I love Deco...for many personal reasons my first visit to this magnificent city has redefined that love, the Grand Hyatt - Hong Kong and especially One Harbour Road with its oh so very 30's feel and ambiance, captures a period...a time when style, art, enjoyment and sheer indulgence were omnipresent. ■ In a city where the very best Chinese food emanates from the lowliest to the loftiest, this quintessence of fine cuisine stands head and shoulders above its peers. ■ When in Rome … in this case Hong Kong, you simply cannot resist the traditional Dim Sum …in this case, the classic Cantonese degustation portions, wontons, buns, and pot-stickers... all overflowing with spicy morsels of chicken beef and pork. Sweet and sour, serious yet fun. ■ Then it's the signal for Chef Li to demonstrate why so many of his peers regard him as one of Hong Kong's leading Cantonese experts. His Baked Crab Meat and Onion in its shell borders on the divine with his Deep- fried Prawns with sesame seed in mayonnaise sauce, a close second. Other examples of his versatility include Braised Spare- ribs in "Wu–Shek" style, Braised Chinese Spinach with mushrooms and deep fried dough, and a house specialty, Fried Rice wrapped with Lotus Leaf. And don't pass on the desserts, especially the Chilled Mango Pudding which made a fitting finale to this exotic feast. ■ "*Miss Otis regrets she's unable to lunch today*" - pity One Harbour Road was not around then Mr. Porter, as I am certain that would have been one engagement she would not have wanted to miss out on!

Top Left

Deep Fried Prawns with Sesame Seeds and Tossed with Mayonnaise

paired with
Rémy Martin V.S.O.P

Bottom Left

Baked Crab Meat and Onion in Shell

paired with
Rémy Martin Extra iced

Above

Mango Pudding

paired with
Rémy Martin Extra iced

One Harbour Road

"There is a tide in the affairs of men, which taken at the flood, leads on to fortune.... On such a full sea are we now afloat. And we must take the current when it serves"- Shakespeare- Julius Caesar.

The Sabatini Brothers, restaurateurs of distinction, are in empire building mode. On the crest of a wave, they have their original Trattoria in Rome (good enough for Federico Fellini- La Dolce Vita and all that. And Pavarotti!) and are taking the Far East by storm, by introducing Sabatini to Hong Kong and Tokyo. ■ Inspired by the late Salvatore *"maestro"* Sabatini (the eldest brother) and the remaining two, Silvestro (a singer of national repute) and Francesco, Sabatini, particularly in Hong Kong, continues to attract an international clientele with truly authentic Roman regional cucina based on classic ancient recipes and developed and presented with flair and ingenuity with the recently appointed Michelin - starred Chef Francesco Brocca. ■ In an environs of true Italian décor faithful to Rome, with smart shades of blue and grey and with a proliferation of objets d'art Italia, Chef Brocca shows off a formidable reputation with a newly created menu of epic proportions – studded with items that remain quintessentially Sabatini - "La Mama" and each very hard to resist! ■ Take your pick, you will find Brocca seems to have most of the answers to your pursuit of the perfect piatti! His antipasti are gems- notably the Chicken Stuffed Vine leaves garnished with Porcini mushrooms and Pine-nut Vinaigrette, and the Mozzarella and Lobster Parcel served with an *"unusual Apple Orange and Fennel salad"*. ■ The entrees, clearly illustrate why the Sabatini brother should be congratulated for their star signing, namely the Oven - baked Whole Dover Sole with lemon, butter and white wine; and the Ossobucco con Funghi- cooked the definitive way - slow braised. Both raise Brocca's game to a subliminal level. ■ The cheese board reveals depth and great knowledge with several hard to get fromaggio della Campagna and of course how else should one finish but with a classic Tiramisu accompanied with a perfectly chilled XO. Multibene! ■ Surely with the Brothers Sabatini, it is a case of *"Veni, vidi vici!"*

Top Left	Top Right
Salmon Tartare	**Linguine with Fresh Seafood**
paired with Rémy Martin V.S.O.P iced	paired with Rémy Martin XO Excellence
Bottom Left	**Bottom Left**
Pan-fried Duck Breast with Sweet and Sour Chocolate Sauce	**Tiramisu / Traditional Mascarpone Cheese Cake**
paired with Rémy Martin Extra	paired with Rémy Martin XO Excellence

...NEW IDEAS...

...old traditions...

Wherever I have traveled in the world, the one thing I have noticed is that just as people, each country has its own unique smell. India ...South Africa... Egypt... France... Japan... China... and the more foreign it is, the more exotic the smell-like an ancient perfume from a thousand years ago. You know instantly where you are and years later, the smell remains vividly in your mind's eye. ■ So it is with Singapore and particularly the beautiful fragrant scents of the orchids (over 60,000) plants and flowers in the Botanical Gardens. I used to play with my brother in those very same gardens. I remember the bold as brass monkeys that used to stroll with lazy arrogance and curiosity - forever on the scrounge. We chased them and then, irritated, they would turn on us, as we fled screaming back to our parents. The monkeys have long gone (W.H.O. and all that!) but the plants and the trees and the flowers remain ... and of course, that beautiful, compelling smell. ■ And so it was with much nostalgia that I found myself in those gardens,....the old house was still there and the hill, on which I chased those saucy simians. It is still a reassuring site and what makes it even more special is the old colonial style building...a pre-war Singapore...gin and tonics...cricket...the Empire of old brigadiers ...and colonels sitting down to dinner...dressed to the nines. All of this is reflected at Au Jardin where grace and charm and an elegance of yesteryear and naturally, style abound. And the food *"ain't"* bad either! ■ Chef Galvin Lim is a very good cook indeed. His efforts at Au Jardin have won him international recognition

"Nothing recalls the past so potently as a smell"— Winston Churchill.

Au Jardin des Amis   ■   Chef Galvin Lim

AU JARDIN DES AMIS

SINGAPORE

and a following.... ■ His Maine Lobster Salad with truffles was perfection manifested - each succulent slice, a salute to taste and freshness - the shaved truffles contributing to the sheer decadence. ■ The entrées are modern renditions of classics that in many ways pay homage to their celebrated award-winning wine list (Thank you Wine Spectator). Of worthy mention is Chef Lim's treatment of Sautéed and Poached Foie Gras in Muscat de Baume de Venise with an Apricot and Raisin Compote...a classic case of intertwining shapes scents and flavors to create balance. Another entrée that fires the imagination and the palate is the Braised Lamb Shank and Sweetbreads, presented with Oven - baked Rack of Lamb. ■ And finally, with the evening drawing in - a selection of cheese from a groaning cheese board to accompany a glass of vintage port... and then of course, giving in to my fondness and a sweet- infused childhood...dessert- in this case a Valrhona Chocolate Molleaux with a praline Ice Cream. ■ *"A trip to the moon on gossamer wings". Cole Porter...Indeed*

Right
Maine Lobster Salad
with Truffle

paired with
Rémy Martin Extra iced

Below
Braised Lamb Shank and
Sweet Bread with Oven-Baked
Lamb Rack

paired with
Rémy Martin XO Excellence

Little did I know that some 50 odd years later I would be whisking a fractious photographer through those very same streets this time in pursuit of the perfect food shot. ■ The colorful taxi came to a halt by the kerb of a very busy street in the height of its rush hour. Pretty girls and crisp-shirted men abounded, chattering and laughing as they made their way home. Bustling Singapore really has not changed one iota in all the time I have been away except for one major area. And that is the Restaurant industry. ■ Then it was the world-renowned Raffles Hotel Grill for the posh and discerning. Alternatively, it was a choice of Chinese, Indian and Malaysian restaurants - all modestly furnished, but very cheap and very, very good. ■ But Asia Pacific and especially Singapore today in the area of haute cuisine has changed and sets the pace for what is happening elsewhere. ■ Les Amis and in particular Chef Justin Quek who developed his considerable talents with French masters including Robuchon, offers exemplary cuisine in the most elegant cutting-edge surroundings...Smart shades of lilac grey and black... sparkling polished glass, and oh! such ultra-chic unforgettable feasting. ■ Quek has it all sussed out, gauging taste flavor and presentation to perfection...The Pan-fried Foie Gras of Duck with its fricassee of mushrooms, truffles sauce and herb salad, was bordering on an out of body experience, as was the Seared Toro a la Nicoise which was a clear reminder of his French sojourns. A Lobster Linguine provided us not only with flavor and texture but also visual pleasure such was the delicate presentation. For pure innovation in balanced flavours however, the Braised Veal Cheek was outstanding. Its accompanying Madeira Sauce adding the aromatic spark that fuelled the taste buds. ■ My appreciation at picking out indulgent sweet things was encouraged in places like Singapore and of course with almost radar-like precision, I zoomed in on Chef Quek's Warm Bitter Chocolate Tart with Banana and Moka Ice Cream – simply marvelous my dear friends! ■ I hope you will discover Singapore's world-class cuisine...It took me close to 50 years, but of course, I am sure your quest will be shorter with similar rewards!

LES AMIS

SINGAPORE

I remember as a little boy hanging onto my parent's hands and whining as they seemingly whisked my older brother Adrian and me through the streets and alleys of post - war Singapore in search of the perfect Satay!

Opposite Page

Top Left
Lobster Linguine

paired with
Rémy Martin
Extra iced

Bottom Right
Braised Veal Cheek,
Madeira Sauce

paired with
Rémy Martin
XO Excellence

Warm Bitter Chocolate Tart With Banana and Moka Ice Cream

paired with
Rémy Martin
Extra iced

Seared Toro a la Nicoise paired with Rémy Martin V.S.O.P chilled lightly

Master Chefs
Jean-Paul Naquin,
Gregoire Simonin &
David Mollicome
(left to right)

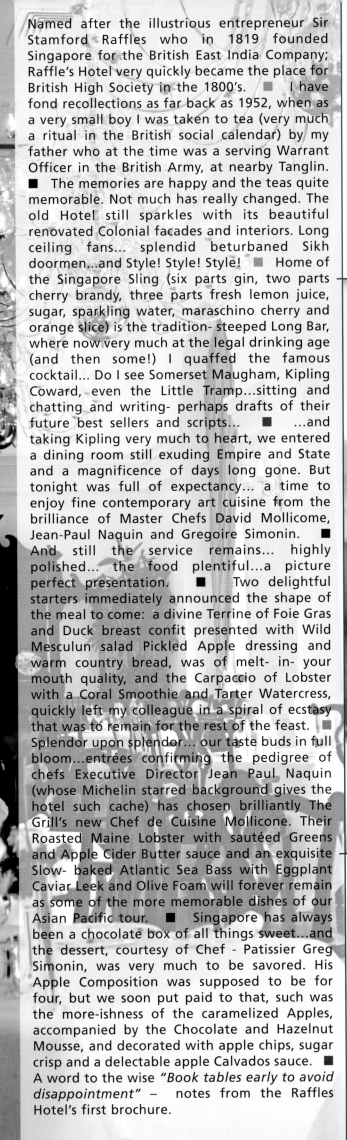

Named after the illustrious entrepreneur Sir Stamford Raffles who in 1819 founded Singapore for the British East India Company; Raffle's Hotel very quickly became the place for British High Society in the 1800's. ■ I have fond recollections as far back as 1952, when as a very small boy I was taken to tea (very much a ritual in the British social calendar) by my father who at the time was a serving Warrant Officer in the British Army, at nearby Tanglin. ■ The memories are happy and the teas quite memorable. Not much has really changed. The old Hotel still sparkles with its beautiful renovated Colonial facades and interiors. Long ceiling fans... splendid beturbaned Sikh doormen...and Style! Style! Style! ■ Home of the Singapore Sling (six parts gin, two parts cherry brandy, three parts fresh lemon juice, sugar, sparkling water, maraschino cherry and orange slice) is the tradition- steeped Long Bar, where now very much at the legal drinking age (and then some!) I quaffed the famous cocktail... Do I see Somerset Maugham, Kipling Coward, even the Little Tramp...sitting and chatting and writing- perhaps drafts of their future best sellers and scripts... ■ ...and taking Kipling very much to heart, we entered a dining room still exuding Empire and State and a magnificence of days long gone. But tonight was full of expectancy... a time to enjoy fine contemporary art cuisine from the brilliance of Master Chefs David Mollicome, Jean-Paul Naquin and Gregoire Simonin. ■ And still the service remains... highly polished... the food plentiful...a picture perfect presentation. ■ Two delightful starters immediately announced the shape of the meal to come: a divine Terrine of Foie Gras and Duck breast confit presented with Wild Mesculun salad Pickled Apple dressing and warm country bread, was of melt- in- your mouth quality, and the Carpaccio of Lobster with a Coral Smoothie and Tarter Watercress, quickly left my colleague in a spiral of ecstasy that was to remain for the rest of the feast. ■ Splendor upon splendor... our taste buds in full bloom...entrées confirming the pedigree of chefs Executive Director Jean Paul Naquin (whose Michelin starred background gives the hotel such cache) has chosen brilliantly The Grill's new Chef de Cuisine Mollicone. Their Roasted Maine Lobster with sautéed Greens and Apple Cider Butter sauce and an exquisite Slow- baked Atlantic Sea Bass with Eggplant Caviar Leek and Olive Foam will forever remain as some of the more memorable dishes of our Asian Pacific tour. ■ Singapore has always been a chocolate box of all things sweet...and the dessert, courtesy of Chef - Patissier Greg Simonin, was very much to be savored. His Apple Composition was supposed to be for four, but we soon put paid to that, such was the more-ishness of the caramelized Apples, accompanied by the Chocolate and Hazelnut Mousse, and decorated with apple chips, sugar crisp and a delectable apple Calvados sauce. ■ A word to the wise *"Book tables early to avoid disappointment"* – notes from the Raffles Hotel's first brochure.

RAFFLES

SINGAPORE

Apple Composition paired with Rémy Martin XO Excellence

"Feed at Raffles" - Rudyard Kipling.

**Lobster Carpaccio,
Tartar of Greens,
Coral Emulsion**

**paired with
Rémy Martin
V.S.O.P iced**

**Sea Bass with Tandoori
Eggplant, Leek and
Olive Oil Dressing**

**paired with
Rémy Martin
Extra iced**

**Burgaud Duck, Cep
Mushroom and Beetroot
Wine Reduction**

**paired with
Rémy Martin Extra**

Raffles

SHANG
PALACE

SINGAPORE

Shang Palace ■
Chef Peter Tsang

Pan-Fried Spare Ribs in
Lemon & Orange Sauce

paired with
Rémy Martin V.S.O.P

Opposite Page

Stir-Fried Crab Meat
with Egg White served
in a Crispy Golden Cup

paired with
Rémy Martin
V.S.O.P iced

Pan-Fried Minced
Shrimps and Cabbage
served with Sweet
& Sour Sauce

paired with
Rémy Martin
XO Excellence

As much as this book is about the art of excellence, so is the definitive cuisine of Master Chef Peter Tsang. Such is his impressive pedigree that he has cooked for Chief Executive Tung Chee Hwa and other world statesmen including Nelson Mandela and Li Peng. ■ I have always maintained that definitive Cantonese Cuisine has its roots and philosophy firmly ensconced in Hong Kong, thus it should come as no surprise that the reason for the stellar reputation of the Shang Palace is that Chef Tsang hails from Hong Kong. ■ With the traditional red overtones and intricate designs including a spectacular butter sculpture, providing a quite dramatic almost theatrical background, Chef Peter Tsang dominates the stage like a Chinese magician with subtle tricks, and legerdemain wizardry! ■ In short the man can cook! He opened this spectacular feast fit for a Ming Imperator with a dazzling array of Dim Sum, the likes of which I swear have no peer in any Chinese restaurant I have ever visited: Steamed Shrimp Dumplings with Bamboo shoots, Steamed Spinach with Garlic Dumplings, Deep-fried Prawn Dumplings, Baked Barbecue Pork Puffs with Sesame-all absolutely delectable! ■ Our taste buds now firmly aroused we awaited more sorcery and yet more magic unfolded with the highly inventive selection of Tang's signature including Pam Fried Spare Ribs in Lemon and Orange sauce (the meat literally falling off the bone!), a quite superlative Stuffed Crabmeat with eggs. (The tender textures nicely pairing with an iced Remy VSOP) and an unbelievable, Pan Fried Minced Shrimps and Cabbage dish served with sweet and sour sauce. ■ Then with almost seamless dexterity, a crash of cymbals with the appearance of the quite exotic, decorative Double Boiled Almond Cream served in a hollowed out fresh Papaya- sheer escapism! ■ The Shangri-La Group of Hotels may boast many fine gourmet restaurants worldwide- indeed some of its finest have made it into this book- but surely right up there and indeed anywhere in the world, the Shang Palace uniquely defines Cantonese cooking at its pinnacle best.

Zensai paired with Rémy Martin V.S.O.P with club soda and ice

SHIRAISHI

SINGAPORE

Chef Shiraishi has no peers. His definitive illustrations of Japanese techniques and presentation are of a world-class level. No surprise that many of today's contemporary chefs borrow from his mastery. ■ Shiraishi quietly dominating his namesake restaurant is only interested in quality. This tiny yet highly exclusive dining room seats only 40 and caters exclusively to the discerning sushi and sashimi gourmet whose criteria likewise is crème de la crème. ■ I have met many world famous chefs and despite their celebrity, I have found them to be regular *"blokes"* generous, kind, centered, unspoiled, sincere. Chef Shiraishi is all of these, as well as having a beautiful personality where serenity and sensitivity are integral. This is manifested in the food he presents. Using the freshest and the best ingredients money can buy (indeed virtually all of the ingredients we sampled came from Tokyo's world-famous Tuskegee market) ■ Watching him hand-shaping and designing his original pieces is a privilege and a very unique experience (imagine if you will watching Rodin sculpting and then you can appreciate the observation). Shiraishi doesn't just prepare his food, he caresses and teases it. The result is nothing short of the spectacularly beautiful. And historic. ■ The shapes and variety of the Zensai selection held great appeal for us, especially the Sesame Bean curd, the Sea Eel Roll with Burdock, The Fried Ginko Nuts, the Deep Fried Prawn with Quail egg and the Grilled Eggplant with Bean paste –all distinctive and all very good! ■ For his next item, Chef Shiraishi offered us the Winter Melon with Shark Fin. This delightful speciality was followed by a succession of the Chef's favorites Shari Su, Sushi Sashiri including the choicest cuts of Sushi, Otoro, Kan Pachi, Maki Ebi, Ikura, Akagai, and Kohada. ■ Desserts by this superb craftsman are a joy to behold as much as savor. The two we were invited to try were indulgence to the max with the Plum Wine Jelly and a Red Bean Paste with Rice cake. ■ I would be curious to see how Michelin would assess this brilliantly aspected restaurant!

Ume Shu Jelly

paired with
Rémy Martin
XO Excellence
on the rocks

Shiraishi ■ Chef Shinji Shiraishi

Sushi

paired with
Rémy Martin V.S.O.P
on the rocks

CITY OF

CONTRASTS

Potato Crepe with Crab and Basil, Potato Puree with Parmesan, and a Caviar Sauce

paired with Rémy Martin V.S.O.P iced

Rack of Lamb in the oven, Cauliflower Pie, a Sw a traditional Mixed Salad from Naples paired with F

Michelin - starred Chef Annie Feolde has created an immense legacy at the original Enoteca Pinchiorri in Florence. Now, thanks to an inspired Executive Chef Toshikazu Tsugi & Chef Olivier, this Tokyo sister has emerged as a world-beater in its own right. ■ Relais and Chateaux is the most discerning organization - a recent survey revealed that it enjoys the highest number of Michelin starred chefs than any other organization. In other words to be part of this elite company, you have to be able to cook a bit, hence Enoteca Pinchiorri's enviable reputation. ■ The busy highly commercial Tokyo street outside is deceiving, for when you enter this magnificent sprawling Ristorante on the top floor, you feel somewhat disoriented- Florentine artifacts abound, Tuscan arches, paintings of Italian life, beautiful table settings in soft pink - so very un-Japanese - so very Rusticana Italiana. Chef Olivier delivers a replica of its older sisters menu in considerable style. Basing his technique in modern Japanese

Trofie tossed with Langoustines and Saffron with a Black Cabbage Pesto and Crispy Potato Ribbons

paired with Rémy Martin Extra iced

**t Bread Sauce and
v Martin XO Excellence**

technique, he sustains the authenticity of Cucina rusticano to immaculate effect. The flavors of a popular seafood sea urchin served with an avocado mousse salad and red wine vinegar with some slices of bruschetta were a heavenly way to start. , As was the item- variation on zucchini served raw marinated and deep-fried – three times the enjoyment guaranteed! ■ Pick of the entrees were two dishes - Potato Crepe with Crab and Basil, together with potato puree with parmesan and a caviar sauce, and a classic rendition of Rack of Lamb in the Oven, with cauliflower pie, sweet bread sauce and a traditional mixed Napoli salad - bellissimo! ■ I notice that the Japanese share the English love for desserts and sweets- so when in Rome as it were, Enoteca Pinchiorri doesn't miss a beat –the assorted Chocolate Dessert plate would have sated the Emperor Lucullus himself. This included personal favorites, a Chocolate Semi- freddo and a Caramel Cremant catching the eye and tantalizing the plate on a plate chock-full of treats! ■ Inspired cooking, Italian flair, impeccable indulgent service- what a wonderful cantata eh?!

Executive Chef Toshikazu Tsugi & Chef Olivier

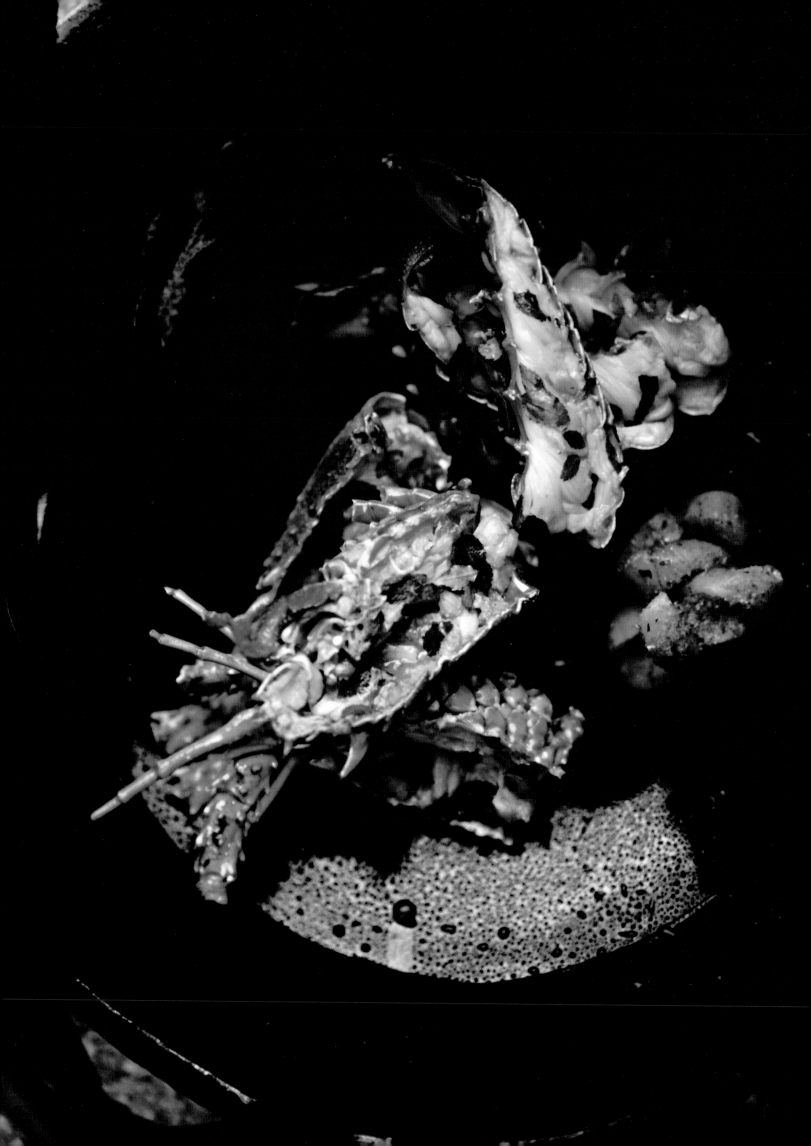

Chef Kenichiro Ooe

"Art is not a special sauce applied to ordinary cooking, it is the cooking itself if it is good" – WR Lethaby- Architect ■ Kenichiro Ooe is both an artist and architect. How appropriate that his chosen stage is here at the magnificent Park Hyatt Tokyo, where every inch of space is dedicated in some way or another to Art. ■ And my, what a rich tapestry from which to draw! Kenichiro Ooe is indeed a remarkably enterprising chef and, whilst clearly committed to a traditional Japanese cuisine, finds many ways of presenting it in a most visual and flavorsome fashion and always with the delicate strokes of the artist's brush ■ With the most dramatic of natural canvasses, Mount Fuji, and with an intelligent siting and design, this exquisite contemporary Japanese restaurant has established a quite formidable reputation with its patrons. ■ The ambient tranquility mirrors the heart of the Japanese people's philosophy, affording a blend of peace and harmony. Subdued earth tones, simple unfussy polished beach tables, thoughtfully set apart, all engage one into enjoying a menu that offers special set meals, or a more extensive a la carte choice of specials. ■ I have always maintained that Japan created true nouvelle cuisine. Ooe not only serves up interesting variations, but also makes dramatically visual use of his serving utensils, where the food on the plate is like an artist's strokes, set against a canvass of beautifully- crafted, earthenware pots, delicate porcelain plates and decorative lacquerware dishes - most of these from fellow local craftsmen. ■ So what about the food- is it remarkable? Our satisfied palates assure a resounding affirmative. The outstanding Pike Eel and vegetables with a jelly will always remain this writer's favorite along with Ooe's other stellar signatures including the Blowfish and Vegetables, dramatically presented in a deep handcrafted pot and a delectable Beef Tongue and Vegetable in a Pumpkin pot. ■ And finally the desserts all tantalizing all so delicious and quite substantial especially the Black Sugar Ice Cream with Sweet Red Bean sauce and the Apple and Soy milk Terrine with Plum sauce. ■ As you would say -Itadaki Masu! (Bon Appetit!)

Grilled Lobster and Soy Sauce

paired with Rémy Martin Extra

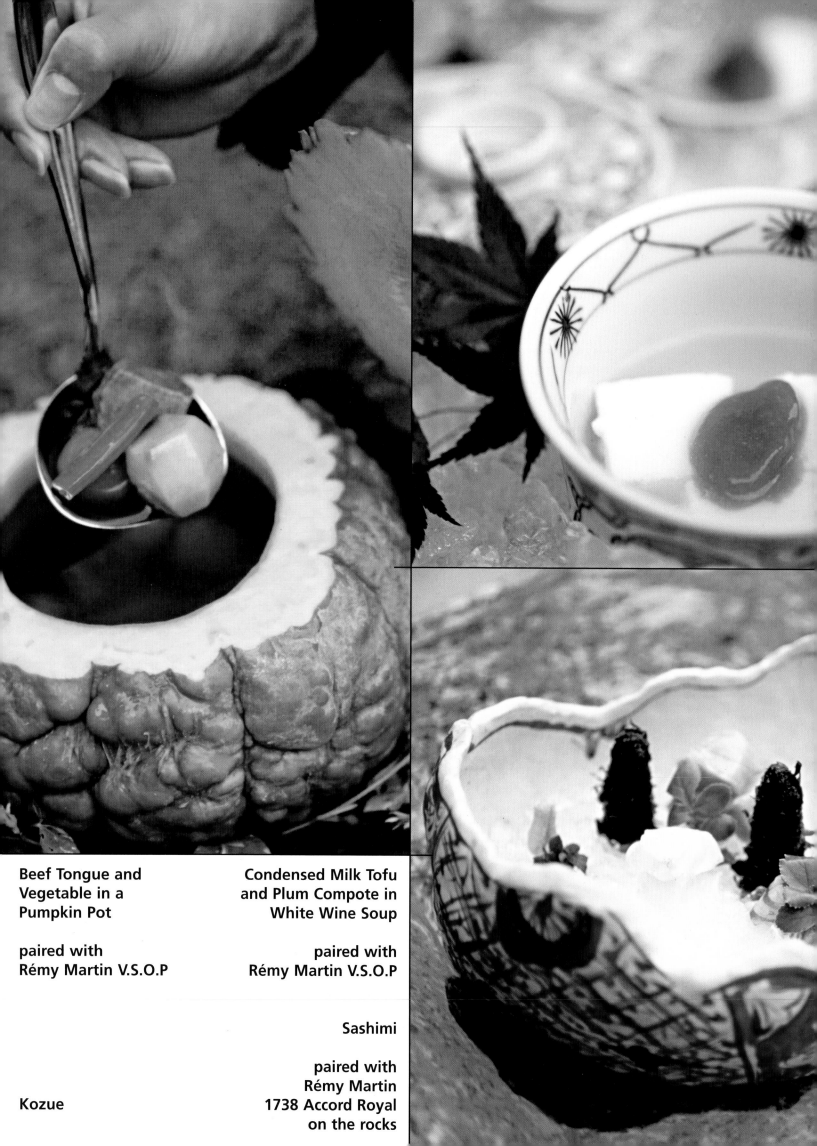

Beef Tongue and Vegetable in a Pumpkin Pot

paired with
Rémy Martin V.S.O.P

Kozue

Condensed Milk Tofu and Plum Compote in White Wine Soup

paired with
Rémy Martin V.S.O.P

Sashimi

paired with
Rémy Martin
1738 Accord Royal
on the rocks

L'ATELIER DE JOEL ROBUCHON

TOKYO

Le Soufflé a la Chartreuse a la Créme Glacée a la Pistache
paired with Rémy Martin 1738 Accord Royal iced

I don't know where it all started, maybe it was made popular by Tetsuya...and even Nobu, but Joel Robuchon, the Grand Master Chef from Lyons, feted for so long by that most stringent of critics, Guide Michelin, is the true pioneer of presenting classic French dishes in degustation portions with traditional Japanese architectural panache. Indeed many of the great Japanese chefs I know have all had their schooling with the old master. ■ Chef Yosuke Suga, no exception at the latest Robuchon innovation L'Atelier de Joel Robuchon, in Tokyo (Robuchon's first!) is a marvel. Learning his lessons well, his presentation is symmetry, color, design, shape, scents and flavors on a tapestry of sheer enjoyment. The palate is beguiled, charmed and entertained, by the scope of this exciting gastronomic concept. Surely this has to be the shape of tastes to come? ■ Plate after plate of inimitable Robuchon signatures appear, sushi bar style, for that's what, in essence, this L'Atelier concept is all about. 40 prime seats in with the action at the sushi-bar kitchen, where the dramatic tones of red and black provide a stunning visual backdrop to the theatrical drama that unfolds, packed night after night. ■ L'Atelier is news, is hot, is chic... and so Tokyo's fashionable Café Society is drawn like a magnet to this voguish establishment in Tokyo's Beverly Hills equivalent. I even shared pleasantries with a visiting chef or two, for such is their professional envy of Robuchon's latest move. ■ And as for the food-wow! ■ Crab cocktail with avocado and fresh coriander...Caviar of Eggplant in a coulis of tangy tomatoes...a crispy Papillote of langoustine with fresh basil...an assortment of Charcuterie ...Caramelized quail with an apple puree - the hits kept on coming. And of course what could follow all of this ... true to the L'Atelier's roots...the ripest of French cheese...and then a spectacular Chartreuse soufflé with a scoop of pistachio ice cream gently sinking into its rich texture - *Voila et merci Chef Yosuke Suga for your dedication to taste!*

Top Left
La Caille Caramelisée avec une Pomme purée

**paired with
Rémy Martin
XO Excellence**

Bottom Left
La Soupe Mimolette

**paired with
Rémy Martin
V.S.O.P iced**

Le Carpaccio de Grosses Crevettes au Graines de Pavot

**paired with
Rémy Martin
V.S.O.P iced**

Chef Toru Kawano

"A lotta cats copy the Mona Lisa, but people still line up to see the original" - Louis Armstrong. ■ Tokyo …the middle of the lunch hour…late August…the weather is hot and humid. There is bustle everywhere, although ordered and oh so polite, one feels the competitiveness of this fast paced metropolis…. ■ Take the elevator to 34th floor of the Yamaguchi building, which respectfully overshadows the emperor's residence… There amongst the most tranquil of surroundings you will find one of Tokyo's truest oases Monna Lisa. The dining room offers elegance, calm style all sweetness and bright bright light. The view of the palace is spectacular. The place though busy retains an atmosphere of profound calm. Perfect to enjoy the Contemporary French classics of the cultured Chef Kawano. ■ No stranger to the disciplines of French Cuisine (he studied under Joel Robuchon), Toru Kawano is a master of true French Classic, but presents them with great delicacy amid an artistry that stems from his Japanese heritage. ■ The dishes are quite brilliant and sparkle with creativity… Grilled Eel with Kidney Beans, Steamed Zucchini Blossoms – appetizers that will create the intrigue necessary to continue on this delightful Franco/Japanese epicurean excursion. ■ The entrées left my colleague weak kneed. He could think of nothing more unique than the Breaded Ayu with cepe and a scent of vanilla. I meanwhile was savoring the textures and shapes of a quite impressive Foie Gras, sautéed with summer vegetables, rich but just too tempting to pass up! ■ And then strike up the band with a symphony of irresistible desserts, composed of a Chocolate decoration of the G Clef on a plate containing a Crème Brulee, Strawberry Cheesecake, Bitter-sweet Chocolate Cake and Red Bean Ice Cream, ■ *I agree with Louis... people will still line up for this one - off!*

MONNA LISA

TOKYO

Left
**Grilled Eel with
Kidney Beans**

paired with
**Rémy Martin 1738
Accord Royal iced**

Right
**Breaded Ayu
with Crepe,
scent of Vanilla**

paired with
**Rémy Martin
V.S.O.P iced**

Monna Lisa

Right
Steamed Quail with
Foie Gras, Wrapped
by Crepe Cabbage

paired with Rémy
Martin 1738 Accord
Royal on the rocks

Left
Symphony of
Desserts

paired with
Rémy Martin
XO Excellence

Sweetbreads with
Shaved Parmesan Cheese

paired with
Rémy Martin V.S.O.P iced

Goose Liver Confit with
Fresh Figs and Cherry
Balsamic Vinegar

paired with
Rémy Martin V.S.O.P iced

**Roasted Lamb
with Burnt Tomato Sauce
and Crispy Zucchini**

**paired with
Rémy Martin
XO Excellence**

NEW YORK
GRILL

TOKYO

What can be more spectacular than the New York Grill with its breathtaking vistas of Tokyo? Tokyo's most popular restaurant, with splashes of colorful murals depicting New York scenes of its legendary sporting institutions and pulsating life-style...halcyon days of a New York...glamour, style and exciting cuisine. ■
The Kiwis are here... precociously talented Chef de Cuisine Matthew Crabbe... the stylish guidance of Executive Chef Brett Patterson...not for a Tokyo second, do these guys miss a trick. Textures and taste that are the very heart and soul of the New York Grill...this high rise theatre of top notch culinary entertainment will have you scaling the headiest of heights. ■ The menu "knocks 'em for dead in the aisles" with a myriad choices that leave you in a wonderful dilemma, but that always guarantees a memorable experience. Memorable moments and memorable dishes are a mélange of compelling starters including a Goose Liver Confit with Fresh Fig, or the Crispy Sweetbreads with Parmesan Risotto. ■ And what about the Grill's staples ... so much for Kobe Beef! The real product is the extraordinary Maesawa Beef, from animals that are as well-fed and pampered as a Sumo wrestler. The result...a feather-light texture and literally as easy to slice as butter, as my sirloin entrée, clearly allowed. My fellow diner has tasted great duck from Singapore to Aylesbury in England, but now, here was a superb offering of Wisconsin Duck

"big" on flavor and "big" in portion, tender, and accented with mango chutney, arugula, tomato salad and a honey soy sauce... ■ I have just arrived having traveled for over 16 hours, but the pulse, the ambience of the New York Grill and Bar, the company of good people like Malcolm Thompson- a brilliant hotelier- with his two stalwarts Messrs. Patterson and Crabbe, and the bright lights of exhilarating Tokyo, provide a wonderful sense of enjoyment as we truly enjoy. ■ In a word -"Captivating!"

Executive Chef Brett Patterson & Chef de Cuisine Matthew Crabbe

"One belongs to New York instantly. One belongs to it as much as in five minutes as in five years" - Thomas Wolfe - US Novelist.

HAPPY   AND
COOKING DOES
ON KNOW-HOW
THE   HEART,
DEMANDS ON T
NEEDS ENTHU
DEEP LOVE OF
IT TO LIFE.

SUCCESSFUL
N'T RELY ONLY
IT COMES FROM
MAKES GREAT
HE PALATE, AND
ASM AND A
OOD TO BRING

GEORGES BLANC, CHEF AND WRITER

AMERICAN

DREAM

"...went into a church..."

CALIFORNIA

"...all the leaves were fallin..."

DREAMING

Tarte au Citron paired with Rémy Martin 1738 Accord Royal

"The great superiority of France over England is that in France every bourgeois wants to be an artist whereas in England every artist wants to be a bourgeois" – *Oscar Wilde.* ■ Picture this...a beret clad figure on a bicycle (pannier and all!) cheerfully whistling as he pedals along a narrow village road. He greets mid-morning strollers with a cheery wave...they wave back in recognition of Yountville's very own French chef... ■ Phillipe Jeanty, both artist and chef, but not bourgeois, is passion personified... His lifestyle, a certain measure of whimsical Gallic eccentricity and a charming handcrafted restaurant, where his

Petit Sale au Lentils

paired with Rémy Martin V.S.O.P

philosophy and flair for hearty paysan fare are so vividly illustrated, all make for a breath of fresh air ...adding to the burgeoning restaurant center that is Yountville in the very heart of the Wine Country. ■ Stepping through the low doorway and waiting briefly for a much-in-demand table, you can appreciate the rusticity of this bistro café, with its quirky interior - all the hard work of Phillipe. With the aproned wait-staff, the oh-so French artifacts and posters, the great smell of cooking and the bustle, well it could be a la champagne! ■ There is nothing pretentious about the menu...Jeanty sticks to the basics and quite simply, he excels. As the word gets out, the lines seem to get longer. His offerings are meant to please, with such classics as Petit Sale Aux Lentilles (Home-cured Belly of Pork with a lentil and Foie gras ragout (his personal favorite!) or another country favorite, Pieds de Cochon (pig's trotters with

Haricot vert Salad) or Rillettes de Canard (Duck and Goat Cheese pate). As for the entrees, a better Cassoulet (done the finite way with white baked beans, lashings of bacon, and studded with duck confit and sausage) you will not find, and the flavorful Quiche Rognons de Veau au Poivre Vert (Veal, Kidneys and Green Peppercorn Sauce) is not to be missed. ■ And what better way to end your pleasant day trip to France than with a memorable Crepes Suzette served with Chantilly and lashings of Cointreau? Voila! Magnifique! Et merci, Monsieur le Chef!

Cassoulet

paired with Rémy Martin XO Excellence

BOUCHON

NORTHERN CALIFORNIA

**Chef
Jeffery Cerciello**

Profiteroles

**paired
with
Rémy
Martin
V.S.O.P**

"I can't afford to die, I'm booked. I'd lose a fortune"-George Burns ■ America's number one Master Chef and restaurant is arguably ... Maestro Thomas Keller and the celebrated French Laundry... Keen to encourage a steady stream of his burgeoning clientele, Keller has installed the talented Jeffrey Cerciello in Bouchon down the road, to cater to those who cannot abide, having to be patient for a chance to secure a booking at

his illustrious flagship and who want to enjoy some tried and trusted Keller signatures at more affordable prices. ■ Chef Cerciello is having fun and so is his staff. Given such free rein from the master, it is no surprise that time and time again Bouchon continues to hit Keller - gold standard. ■ Bouchon is boisterous and unashamedly rive gauche...Shades of Van Gogh's Grand Fin de Siecle Montmartre...a busy well stocked bar...reading sticks...huge back mirror...sweeping potted palms...Remy and Ricard...bustling waiters and...food glorious food. Piping hot at pop prices...and above all no wait! ■ And oh so very place des artistes and very French...Terrine de Foie Gras - delivered with a degree of Gallic panache and in a pot with lashings of toast points...! Soupe de l'Oignon, Boudin Blanc, Steak Frites, Croque "Madame" (a variation!) A superbly cooked and presented Cabillaud Piperade, and very anti-Atkins Diet desserts including the decidedly indulgent Profiteroles and

**Cabillaud
Piperade**

**paired
with
Rémy
Martin
1738
Accord
Royal
chilled**

a quite wicked Mousse au Chocolate Noir. ■ The pavement terrace is a favorite spot where, on a very balmy late summer evening, over a carafe of house wine and some post-dinner cheese and port, one can linger, watching the time pass, as the sun slowly spread its rays over the quaint thoroughfare that is Washington Street Yountville ...In my mind's eye, I could almost hear the bells of Sacre Coeur and Colette's Paris beckoning me...

Top Left
The French Laundry

Top Right
Chef Thomas Keller

Terrine of
Duck Foie Gras
paired with
Rémy Martin
XO Excellence

**Roasted Squab Breast filled with Foie Gras & Truffles
paired with Rémy Martin 1738 Accord Royal**

With hints of Gascony (part of his heritage) here, Morocco there, and all in the magic Arabesque sweeps and swirls of the rich vibrant colors of a stylish tent-like dining room, Hubert Keller maintains his high-profile consistency to the max. Serving intricate renditions of Classic French cuisine, Chef Keller, together with charming wife Chantel, excels in bringing a discerning taste to the discriminating San Franciscan community. ■ Keller, these days, in his newly remodeled and refitted dining room, like the speed and thrills he gets from his beloved Harley motorbikes throttles up like a thoroughbred racer. His successes under

Warm Golden Rhubarb Tart

paired with Rémy Martin XO Excellence

the watchful eyes of Grand Masters Bocuse and Verge and his working in the kitchen of Michelin-starred establishments have defined both his craft and his willingness to take risks. He could fall off the saddle at any time but he doesn't. Spectacular presentation coupled with subliminal taste reveals a personal favorite of Foie Gras - this time a treatment of a "Duo of Hudson Valley Duck Foie Gras Bartholdi" (Baeckeoffe of foie gras, truffles fingerling potato coupled with seared duck burger and foie gras in a brioche bun). Equally appealing as a starter is the Roasted Maine Lobster with a distinctive artichoke puree citrus salad with a drizzle of Porcini oil. ■ His entrees are sheer gastronimique indulgence. Of note are the Seared Dayboat Scallops with melted blinis and leeks served with lobster and parsnips Ossetra caviar and a corn sauce with vanilla bean; and the Squab dish, this time presented as Roasted Squab Breast filled with foie gras and

truffles, with a ravioli of squab leg confit and finished with a Sauternes ginger sauce. ■ His slender elegant frame belies his passion for all things sweet (Francois Payard eat your heart out!) with a top ten list of classics desserts. Like the grand old master Escoffier, Keller's denouement is a selection of such treats as the Warm Golden Rhubarb Tart served on Sauternes Crème Anglais with ginger vanilla ice cream, and an impeccable Warm Chocolate and Walnut Crépe *"en dentelle"* with dark chocolate sorbet and chocolate and banana pot de crème. ■ Allez les bleus!

Roasted Main Lobster

paired with Rémy Martin V.S.O.P

MASA'S

NORTHERN CALIFORNIA

New ideas and innovative concepts are afoot, under the formidable helmsmanship of "Iron Chef" Ron Siegel (he won his spurs with French Laundry and Daniel). Basing his creativity on the original visionary concepts of the founder, Siegel has added a further dimension to contemporary French - based cooking. The result is perfectly positioned against a striking backdrop of designer Orlando Diaz-Azcuy's elegantly chic interior. ■ A seasonally changing menu of enterprising freshness, in both content and flavor, is in store for the aficionado of all things quality. Choosing from four special menus, including degustations ranging from three to nine courses, or a prix-fixe menu, which includes dessert and coffee, you will encounter unusual and decidedly seductive starters, especially the prix-fixe, where the Pan Seared Artisan Foie Gras, with spicy poached Santa Rosa plums, peach reduction with a brioche crouton, and a delectable soft-shell crab, with champagne mango and red onion

Squab Breast

paired with Rémy Martin V.S.O.P

chutney and cucumber – water, infused with cilantro, are the pick. ■ Highlights of an ambitious array of entrees, include King Salmon with a fiery pesto and Provencal – Styled Ratatouille, with heirloom tomato sauce and if game is your "bag", then try the Sonoma Duck Breast, generously portioned with daikon, bok choy, sugar snap peas, pickled Santa Rosa plums and duck jus. Both are quite spectacularly presented and exquisite - tasting. ■ Desserts, by veteran Patissier Keith Jeanminette, are offbeat

Maine Lobster paired with Rémy Martin 1738 Accord Royal

interpretations of the classics. To a great extent, this novel and whimsical approach works most of the time, especially his innovative Peach Melba with raspberry coulis, crème fraiche ice cream and the absolutely irresistible Strawberry Brioche with buttermilk pannacotta and berry sorbet. And if that doesn't herald the end of your "Siegel Spectacular".... there is a selection of the lovingly hand-crafted petit fours... ■ *We know Masa must be smiling!*

ANTONELLO

SOUTHERN CALIFORNIA

Rated by Zagat as the *"best Italian restaurant in Orange County,"* Antonio Cagnolo's establishment is like the proverbial candle, as it continues to draw a decidedly indulgent and chic Southern Californian crowd. ■ The purely theatrical setting and music from the *"old country"* add to the authentic Italian atmosphere. Antonello is a classic combination of both fun and romance, and it is here that you feel the timelessness and warmth of Northern Italy. If it is tranquillity that you seek, then opt for one of the many private dining rooms, which range from the rustic to the stately in theme. ■

Antonio's passion is evident in the food he serves but also in his love for art. Indeed, many works of his good customer and friend, Aldo Luongo, lend spectacular whimsy to the proceedings. ■ But do not forget the inspirational menu, which is a true celebration of Antonio's origins *"the escarpments of Italy."* From the dazzling array of appetizers, including a signature Bresaola con Soncino e Arugula, that

literally *'melts in your mouth'*, and an exemplary Porcini Soufflé, made to order with the freshest Fontina cheese and served with a truffle oil sauce.... From a full range of pasta, risotto and filet mignon to an inspirationally sublime dessert cart... Whatever your fancy, it is highly unlikely that you will be disappointed with the inspired cooking of Executive-Chef and currently California's *"Chef of the*

Year" (Bellissimo!) Franco Barone. ■ As for the grand finale...make sure you reserve your order, as an indulgent and enthusiastic master patissier offers classics including a simply wondrous Grand Marnier Chocolate Soufflé Cake - tantalizingly served hot with a scoop of vanilla bean ice-cream! ■ And speaking of performances, for you avid South Coast Performing Arts attendees, you can comfortably enjoy a reasonably priced pre-theatre menu, before being whisked away by the complimentary shuttle, in time for *"curtain up"* at the nearby center.

Porcini Soufllé paired
with Rémy Martin V.S.O.P

Vitello Alla Saltimbocca
paired with Rémy Martin XO Excellence

Grand Marnier Chocolate Soufflé Cake
paired with Rémy Martin Extra

Ravioli Di Granchio All'Imperiale
paired with Rémy Martin V.S.O.P

**Filo wrapped Shrimp Mousse paired
with Rémy Martin 1738 Accord Royal chilled**

CRUSTACEAN

SOUTHERN CALIFORNIA

The An Dynasty has come full circle in a story that evolved, just before the fall of Saigon, in San Francisco in 1971, with the smash hit success of Thanh Long, their American Dream was realized in 1991 with the opening of Crustacean in San Francisco then this their flagship in Beverley Hills, in 1997, and finally their new supper-club concept in Vegas, Prana. ■ So what sustains this magic circle of achievement? ■ The secret to its worldwide recognition is simply Helene An's resolve to maintain the mysteries of her "secret kitchen"...an area kept entirely separate from the rest of the restaurant and where only the family has access...here that all the unique flavors that make up their intriguing dishes are created from recipes that have been handed down from generation to generation. ■ An's sophisticated fusing of French, Chinese and Vietnamese influences is apparent ..."*Asian Tapas*"...Fresh Salmon Seared and wrapped in crispy filo, with a chili soy dipping sauce... tantalizing Light Puff Pastries filled with Dungeness Crab and Comte Francais, accompanied with a peanut mustard emulsion... wholly satisfying New Zealand Green Lip Mussels, broiled with

Asian pesto and served with seasoned crostini... ■ The Lite Vegetarian Series menu - a direct influence of the founder's training in Asian herbal medicine-, is also a *"must sample"* - especially the Ragout of Fresh Eggplant, Italian pear tomatoes with tofu, tossed with Vietnamese herb *"Tia–to"*...quite appealing to the eye with its presentation in an earthenware crock. ■ The pleasure continues with such choices as Cornish Hen, spit-roasted, with Asian vegetables, mushrooms and Pappy Van Winkles' Remy glaze, and the no - nonsense French - inspired Grilled Rack of Lamb with roasted potatoes and mixed greens and suddenly a hitherto quietly indulgent meal is sensationally transformed into a veritable feast fit for an emperor. ■ And then it's *"music sweet music"* with desserts that will knock your designer-socks off as you spoil yourself ...especially with a volcanically extravagant Chocolate Lava Cake filled with molten rich - as - Croesus - chocolate and topped with vanilla bean ice-cream and whipped cream. Meeoww! ■ Truly for the family An, the world is very much their oyster!

Top Right
Cornish Hen Spit Roasted paired with Rémy Martin V.S.O.P on the rocks

Bottom Left
Chocolate "Lava" Cake paired with Rémy Martin XO Excellence

LA CACHETTE

SOUTHERN
CALIFORNIA

Soufflé

**paired
with
Rémy Martin
V.S.O.P
chilled**

"The Iron chef with a velvet touch" is celebrity Chef Jean Francois Meteigner and his complete understanding of food. Truly a Hemingwayesque character - he is very much his own man-preferring the solitude of hunting and fishing. Above all, like Hemingway, he keeps his art simple, but throughout his many classic samples of Cuisine Moderne, there is a complexity and depth to his use of ingredients and presentation where color and harmony are everything. Indeed so sensual is the final plate that even that bete noire of restaurateurs - critic Irene Verbilas - was quick to dub his food *"sexy"*! ■   La Cachette is uncompromisingly a tribute to Meteigner's French origins. This little building nestling so discretely in this LA backwater has won accolades from far and wide. Pretty is a word that is rarely used but one that is so apt when describing the charming cottage-like interior with a huge fireplace as its focal point. ■   Meteigner reaffirms his status with starters of infinite variety; House-Smoked Mesquite Atlantic Salmon with little corn cakes, caviar and condiments...Jean Francois Duck Foie Gras Terrine seasoned Black pepper and Muscat wine and served with Brioche toast. More Meteigner magic follows with his entrees. The more noteworthy (and many are very close to perfection) are a truly original presentation of Seared Alaskan Black Cod with ginger plum sauce, Grilled Ratatouille and a mango - papaya relish (shades of Gauguin?) And a quite enterprising treatment of game; his Seared Marinated Venison Chop in a game blueberry

**Seared
Alaskan
Black Cod**

**paired
with
Rémy Martin
1738 Accord Royal**

sauce served with Red Yam Tower and Roasted Chestnut.   ■ Naturally it would be folly to depart this gastronomic odyssey without indulging in the house desserts. Two, to coin UK food reviewer Michael Winner's (he of Deathwish fame!) favorite expression, could be described as historic - the Provencal Apricot Tart with caramel sauce (allow thirty minutes for maximum delight!) And his special treatment of an old classic, Cinnamon Crème Brulee topped with crunchy hazelnut caramel and fresh berries... *Voila! Helas!*

**Napoleon of Sautéed Foie Gras & Foie Gras Terrine
paired with Rémy Martin 1738 Accord Royal iced**

PAVILION

SOUTHERN CALIFORNIA

Chef Laurent Méchin

French-born chef, Laurent Méchin, who was valedictorian at the Gevigney Culinary School near Paris where he was trained, served an apprenticeship at L'Auberge de Chavannes, a Michelin starred establishment. His energy and enthusiasm is still apparent, despite the fact he is a 20-year veteran of the industry. Consistently ranked by the Zagat Survey as one of the Top Ten Restaurants in Southern California for food, décor and service, Pavilion continues as a local favorite. With spectacular ease, Chef Laurent has adjusted the menu to reflect his style without compromising signature dishes. ■ And thus the greatest show in Southern California enjoys its extended run...The continuing accolades are myriad...Wine Spectator Award for Excellence...1999, Di RoNA (ninth consecutive year!) Zagat (number 1 in Orange County 2002). Méchin has vision and talent that unerringly hits the mark with an inspired eclectic cuisine - so much in keeping with the discerning palates of a well-heeled group of the area's

"movers and shakers". ■ Dining here is one of life's great pleasures...a veritable oasis of such tranquility...that the hustle and bustle of neighboring Fashion Island, a landmark mall, seems light years away. Lush floral exotica, artwork and an airy dining room are the constituents of a most memorable experience. ■ The dinner menu is impressive with classic signatures, such as a compelling Seared Rare Ahi Tuna with wasabi and sweet chilli vinaigrette and an enticing Lightly-Spiced Corn

Chowder with smoked shrimp, and celebrated entrees, such as Seared Norwegian Salmon with wild rice, baby fennel in a Chardonnay dill sauce or the well-received, Pepper Crusted Roasted Colorado Lamb with mashed potatoes and a port wine reduction. And for the figure-conscious, perhaps the thoughtfully created Wild Mushrooms and Spinach Cannelloni with oven-dried tomato and Porcini cream. ■ Desserts add a dash of frivolity to the formal surroundings, with Apple Tarte Tatin – a caramelized apple tart with Calvados honey

ice cream; and a-to-die-for, Fondue Chocolate Cake with molten Valrhona dark chocolate, white chocolate sorbet and sour cherry sauce. ■ Méchin, a native of Gascon, France, has earned his 5-star right to rule with creative displays and a panache reminiscent of many of the Michelin - starred super chefs from the grand salles of Paris. Prenez garde Robuchon, Senderens, Ducasse et al, there is much of France, right here in America's own backyard.

Opposite Page

Top Left
Pepper Crusted Rack of Colorado Lamb paired with Rémy Martin 1738 Accord Royal

Top Right
Terrine of Duck Foie Gras "Brulée" paired with Rémy Martin V.S.O.P on the rocks

Bottom Left
Sautéed Jumbo Prawns paired with Rémy Martin V.S.O.P on the rocks

Bottom Right
Banana Créme paired with Rémy Martin XO Excellence

**Stuffed Breast of Quail and seared
Foie Gras with Chanterelles paired
with Rémy Martin XO Excellence**

There'll be dancing in the street with our children at our feet, and tomorrow that we worshipped will be gone " Peter Townsend. The Who - "Won't get fooled again" ■ Packed to the seams night after night in conditions that are essentially close encounters of an extraterrestrial kind, Wunderkind and sometime drummer, Chef Paul Kahan, lays down a rock steady beat as he drives his inspired Culinary version of Contemporary Rhythm and Blues to chart topping heights. Paul Kahan doesn't seduce - he

Seared Mediterranean Dorade

paired with Rémy Martin 1738 Accord Royal chilled

startles, in the vein of the inspired genius of a Keith Moon or a Jon Bonham. ■ And all for the pleasure of a chic group of beautiful faces as the buzz soars in crashing crescendos. ■ His stage is set against the stark interior backdrop of white walls and oblique angles, which perversely sits comfortably with the staccato edginess of hip cooking at its dynamic best. ■ The rivet cymbal is in steady stream as Kahan starts to build a virtuoso solo as he opens his act with a selection of appetizers; Sautéed Veal Sweetbreads with black mission figs, honey butter and golden beets (probably from Kahan's real labor of love- his garden at home). Another soft pedal on the hi-hat and we witness a Crisp Sucking Pig with red grapes and a slaw of grilled bitter greens, celery and fennel. ■ Then it's a double paradiddle of a Seared Mediterranean Dorade with haricots verts, champagne grapes, buckwheat crepe, parsley and verjus, in synch with the Stuffed Breast of Quail and Seared Foie Gras.

with chanterelles sour cherries baby leeks and cherry gastrique … oh music sweet music there'll be music every where... ■ And then as the solo reaches its climax a series of drives on the crash with some nifty footwork on the bass pedal with the White Chocolate Mint ice cream sandwich with pepper mint bark and orange soda and a Plum Ginger Upside-down Cake with vanilla bean ice-cream (so... I like ice-cream!) ■ Keith Moon eat your heart out... ■ *This is Paul Kahan's Magic Bus!*

Sauted Veal Sweetbreads

paired with Rémy Martin XO Excellence

Like the skillful yachtsman he is, Sandro Gamba has set his course for Culinary Paradise and once he sets sail you know that your expedition will be of the highest epicurean standards. ■ Gamba's precocious talents have been developed through several exotic ports of call, including Lespinasse at the St Regis NYC, Louis XV in Paris with Ducasse, Le Jamin with Robuchon and Le Moulin de Mougins with Verge. ■ Now firmly at the helm of one of Chicago's landmark icons, Gamba's daily offerings are presented with poise, elegance and a quiet passion. His plates are as breathtaking as the heart stopping views of the historic Water Tower and the mighty Lake Michigan from the modernistic contemporary environs of NoMi (North of Michigan). ■ The view is breathtaking at breakfast, lunch or dinner, but if you're fortunate enough to be seated at twilight, you'll be entranced by fifteen minutes of piercing blue light that seeps through the sloping floor-to-ceiling bay windows of NoMI. It's the final transformation of day into

night and it's one of those single moments that should be captured in a glass jar and preserved forever. ■ But Chef Gamba's eyes focus on another view. Presented on stage is an elegant display of French and Japanese culinary dishes ranging from melt-in-your-mouth sushi and sashimi, Rotisserie Rack of Summerfield Lamb, with eggplant and roast pepper terrine, potato fondant and Taggiasca olive lamb jus, to a Halibut Confit in olive oil with tomato jam papparadelle of zucchini and 8 year vinaigrette. And all are worthy of display in the Chicago Museum of Contemporary Art. ■ The presentation of food is graceful, sophisticated and yet astonishingly clean and simple. The design of the restaurant unfolds from a 3,000 bottle wine cellar to a bar lounge, which opens up to the sleek and minimalist styled dining room. The walls are decorated with works from such masters as Gerhard Richter, Isamu Noguchi, and Dale Chihuly, adding the final finishing touches to the artist's palette.

Rotisserie Rack
of Summerfield
Lamb

paired with
Rémy Martin
1738 Accord
Royal

NoMi ■ Chef Sandro Gamba

Top Right
**Roasted Wild
King Salmon**

paired with
Rémy Martin
V.S.O.P chilled

Bottom Left
**Chocolate Gaufrettes
with Pur Caraibe
Chocolate Veloute**

paired with
Rémy Martin
Louis XIII

D
A
L
L
A
S

... ONLY COWBOYS?

THE FRENCH ROOM

DALLAS

**La Belle
Farms Squab
& Foie Gras**

**paired
with
Rémy Martin
Extra**

"To eat is human, to digest ...divine!" - Charles T Copeland ■ Prepare yourself for a sensory overload as you enter one of the city's most revered restaurants, The French Room. Located inside the Beaux-Arts style Hotel Adolphus built in 1912, The French Room is as much a feast for the eyes as the classic cuisine is for the palate. A Cathedral-like ceiling mural by Alexandra Rosenfield crowns the room with rosy-cheeked cherubs, pale blue skies and clouds embellished by gilded Rococo arches and a stunning hand blown crystal chandelier. ■ Since 1994, the charismatic Executive Chef William A. Koval has been keeping the

French/American cuisine contemporary and fresh. Amidst the detailed beauty of the décor, Koval, like the perfectionist he is, strives to create food that is elegant yet simple, paying attention to matching flavors on one plate. The Fresh Norton Sound King Crab, Crawfish and Jumbo Lump Crab Salad, for example is a delicately presented arrangement of king crab meat and fresh crawfish with a contrepoint of curry-mayonnaise creating perfect harmony with the sweetness of the roasted beets and the added fusion of the frozen curry cream. The combination of flavors is divine. Equally recommended is the Lemon-poached Maine Lobster, with the unusual saffron-colored lobster mushrooms, and a puree of fava beans in a quite enticing white truffle tomato sauce. ■ Of the main courses, the Pan Seared La Belle Breast of Squab is succulent and with the added indulgence of the Foie Gras and a sliver of bacon - wholly impressive -

**Red Norton
Sound King
Crab**

**paired
with
Rémy Martin
1738 Accord
Royal iced**

served with a braised red cabbage, glazed apple and sweet squab reduction, it was the pick of the entrees - which also included an unusual creation of Sweet White Miso, marinated Alaskan Halibut with Shiitake, spinach sweet potatoes and a carrot ginger sauce. Thoroughly swept away by the impeccable service, the exquisite cuisine and awesome surroundings, we see the only way to improve upon a near perfect evening is to try the culinary Calypso of Coriander and Vanilla poached Pineapple with coconut streusel and coconut sorbet in a pineapple reduction – the perfect ending to a fairy tale evening.

Coriander & Vanilla Poached Pineapple with Coconut Streusel paired with Rémy Martin Extra lightly chilled

Top Left
North Dakota
Buffalo Steaks paired
with Rémy Martin V.S.O.P

Bottom Right
Duo of Banana
Desserts paired
with Rémy Martin
1738 Accord Royal
lightly chilled

Bottom Left
Bahia Magdalena
Baja California Scallop
paired with Rémy Martin
XO Excellence

"I'm going to catch that horse if I can. And when I do I'll give her my brand. And we'll be friends for life, I'll treat her like a wife...I'm going to catch that horse... I'm going to catch that horse if I can! " - The Byrds - Roger McGuinn, Gram Parsons, Dave Crosby, Gene Parsons and Chris Hillman. ■ He likes singing in a band, Lucchese Boots (hand made, of course!) Robert E. Lee and Gram Parsons (ex-Byrds). He's cooked for queens and

presidents as much as the gourmet regular and was once described as the *"founding father of southwestern cuisine."* It was one Craig Claiborne, who first noticed his precocious work and thus a star was born. Today, Dean Fearing is recognized by many of his illustrious contemporaries and his adoring clientele as the heart and soul of the 5 Diamond Award-winning Mansion on Turtle Creek. ■

Fearing has no fear when it comes to innovation with his beloved Southwestern cuisine. As much eclectic as indigenous, he's a Mr. Perpetual Motion when it comes to presentation, textures and flavors. Home - grown spices, herbs and ingredients are the nature of his game and he is at the top of it. ■ As a counterpoint to this extrovert, is the Mansion itself with its stately decor, an absolutely appealing conservatory overlooking the pretty gardens... a case of *"this*

mansion having a sweet and pleasant air". ■ But what a culinary performance! ■ The famed Mansion Tortilla Soup with chicken avocado and cheddar cheese - in a word extraordinary! An indigenous Warm Lobster Taco with yellow tomato salsa and Jimica salad and then two entrées - The Bahia Magdalena Scallops with Canadian chanterelle, mushroom sauce on a compote of summer peas, Fava Beans and Basil with

Chef Dean Fearing

Prosciutto-Wrapped Asparagus, and his classic Chilean Sea Bass with pueblo corn crust on crabmeat with white cheddar hash and ranchero tangerine sauce. All had us tripping on Dean's *"magic swirling ship"* on a voyage of historic shapes tastes and flavors... ■ ... what a rich tapestry this *"oh-so-cool"* master craftsman weaves...and well worth the detour!

MANSION ON TURTLE CREEK DALLAS

MIAMI

SPICE

AZUL

MIAMI

**Truffle Steamed Bass
Wrapped in Buttery
Cabbage
paired
with
Rémy Martin
V.S.O.P iced**

Page 145

Chef
Michelle
Bernstein

Some like it hot...Miami is hot...Azul - cool blue accents and an abundance of water, inside and out, notwithstanding - is hot... Michelle Bernstein, that petite and oh so pretty, culinary ingénue, is hot, making me liking it hot... ■

"Age cannot wither, nor custom stale, the infinite variety" of Ms Bernstein... Some chefs work hard and some chefs are simply brilliant who make it look easy... Bernstein is that chef of rare quality and exception who both works hard and cooks with passion and brilliance...

Her charismatic appeal had this writer completely under her spell as she presented dishes of compelling beauty and flavor. ■ Bernstein does not just attract your palate - she seduces it with all the wiles of a modern day Helen launching a thousand ships of sublime tastes and flavors to carry you on an odyssey to paradise. She is the ultimate Diva who dominates her home turf, having cooked with such masters as Norman Van Aken and Daniel Boulud and then astonishing the dining world with her sensual productions at her own restaurants at The Strand in South Beach. ■ As befits this ex-ballerina's stage, behind the open theatre kitchen of a chicly designed split level Azul, Bernstein is pure poetry in motion. In short the girl can cook. ■ This is no hype flash-food – in-a-pan-poseur, that one sees in the faddish so-called celebrity chefs...a presentation of a starter of Chocolate "Mole" painted foie gras accented with Italian Amarena cherries with cherry gastric was an opening statement of substance and sensitivity. Her artist's soul was impressionably exposed with a signature pas de deux of beguiling entrees; a rare treatment of Quail, filled with morels and lobster, Striped Bass Truffle steamed and delicately wrapped in a crisply finished savoy cabbage. ■ Her piece de resistance, in keeping with the traditions of the legendary grand masters was a dessert of Fire-Roasted Peach with pistachio ice cream and a twist of mango tuille...all that was missing was a shower of red, red, roses... but the florist had closed!...Bravo!

Quail
Filled
with
Morels
and
Lobster

paired
with
Rémy Martin
V.S.O.P
chilled

Roasted
Peach
with
Pistachio
Ice Cream

paired
with
Rémy Martin
XO Excellence

CAFFÉ ABBRACCI

FLORIDA

Enter the vivacious world of Caffe Abbracci, where true to his native Venezie, Nino Pernetti continues to bring us the delicate shapes and flavors that are such a quintessential part of that region's classic dishes. ■ Coral Gables has gradually become the Epicurean center of South Florida and Caffe Abbracci has played a great part in that story. The coveted AAA Five Diamond Award, amongst the many accolades are a testimony to a commitment to perfection. ■ The interior's combination of stunning burl wood ceilings, a profusion of blooms and green

Bocconcino

paired with Rémy Martin Extra

marble accents, offer a backdrop of romance. Step into the intimate bar and you are part of the nightly soiree of South Florida's *'beautiful people.'* ■ A stellar team, headed up by Chef and Partner Mauro Bazzanini, offers an array of dishes that embrace the flavors for which this region is lauded. The signature starter, Bocconcino Abbracci is a must, a specialty of melted mozzarella and topped with porcinis, white wine, and capers. As for the Fresh Goose Liver sautéed in walnut oil, balsamic vinegar and pinenuts and served on a bed of wild rice and chopped Portobello mushrooms - heady food, indeed. ■ Risotto dishes are a test of true Italian fare and disappointingly, even the better restaurants tend to over elaborate what is basically paysan staple food. However, my skepticism soon dissolved with my first taste of the Asparagus and Champagne Risotto, prepared just as it appeared on the menu. Also of note was an outstanding

Lamb Chops, Seared baby lamb chops

paired with Rémy Martin Extra

Dover Sole with Lemon, sautéed in prosecco wine, light fish stock, and capers. ■ And what Italian meal is complete without dolci? Don't leave without trying the freshly made Tiramisu and an absolutely enticing Cannoli Siciliano. These much-abused desserts deserve gentle treatment and a receptive palate. Both were much in evidence at our sitting, where the authentic flavors and the delicate sponge confirmed the decision to dine here. ■ ...Venice really doesn't seem so far away!

Cannoli Siciliano paired with Rémy Martin XO Excellence

Grilled Caribbean Lobster paired with Rémy Martin Extra

**Grilled Conch
Ceviche with
Avocado Butter**

**paired with
Rémy Martin
V.S.O.P**

MARK'S
LAS
OLAS

FLORIDA

"But did thee feel the Earth move"-Ernest Hemingway ■ A people-watcher of a restaurant that oozes sex appeal and narcissistic bustle, more like Manhattan than the Miami down the road...flashy cars that cruise the streets ...beautiful people who walk them...mingling here with the perfect blend of sleek sophistication and a hip savvy attitude...a cocktail here, a cigar there ... shades of Hemingway...this is the style of Mark's Las Olas! ■ Located in trendy downtown, Mark's is most certainly the place to be and be seen. Serving perfectly presented Mediterranean/American cuisine, predominantly seafood, Chef/Owner Mark Militello and Executive Chef Stefan Boillon have captured in their items the concept that less is most definitely more. The Grilled Conch Ceviche, for example, seductively served in a most appropriate Martini glass, is the perfect aperitif to the feast that awaits you. Prepared with olives, avocado, lettuce, red bell peppers, red onion and a myriad spices, is an elegant choice – delicate yet flavorful this perfect pairing of ingredients is both healthy and light. And entrees ... get your taste buds soaring...coming from the depths of the Ocean...in metaphysical contrast...the Grilled Caribbean Lobster, basted with a ginger-mango brown butter and served over West Indian pumpkin rice - typically tropical, Man! Or a sensuous Zucchini and Prosciutto Wrapped Snapper with saffron whitewater clams and fingerling potatoes... both dishes encompassing Militello's and Boillon's desire to create a refined

world-class menu in a hip and happening environment. ■ Just outside of the main room, you can dine on the terrace and gaze at the passing street life... It's a choice spot to indulge in one of Patissiere Katie Holt's decadent desserts.... in particular, an indulgent Passion Fruit Pudding Cake with blueberry confit and lychee sorbet. ■ Super-suave, super-sharp, and sumptuously delicious, Mark's has become a welcoming home for an eclectic crowd of trendsetters, devout gourmets, and celebs alike. And Militello has certainly paved the way for sleek yet serious restaurants in Florida.

**Zucchini & Prosciutto
Wrapped Snapper
with Saffron,
Whitewater Clams**

**paired with
Rémy Martin
Extra**

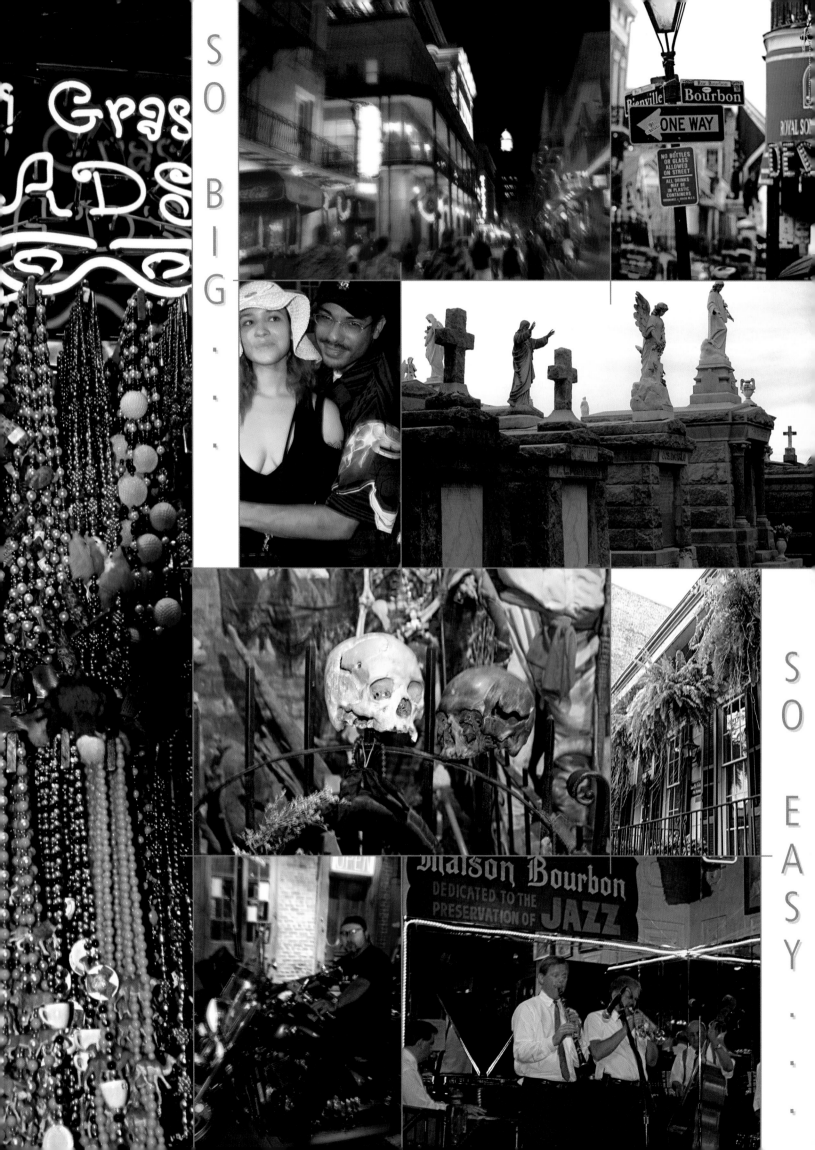

CHRISTIAN'S

NEW ORLEANS

Christian's ■ **Chef Michel Focqeteau**

OPPOSITE PAGE

Top
Crawfish Carolyn

**paired with
Rémy Martin
V.S.O.P iced**

Center
Skip

**paired with
Rémy Martin 1738
Accord Royal**

Bottom
Baby Veal "Christian"

**paired with
Rémy Martin XO
Excellence with a
splash of water**

"Who would marry Rita for her cooking?!"- Dick Haymes (when asked at his wedding if Rita Hayworth had ever cooked for him) ■ And so it came to pass that Christian Ansel and Hank Bergeron, were looking for a new restaurant when they came upon this Lutheran Church and lo, one year later it opened and even the critics saw that it was good. ■ Soon there came a chef, from France, with a desire to make this marriage of food and wine a good thing. Inspired by the goodness around him, he set forth in his kitchen, producing wondrous things...things of beauty...things of taste...shape... texture and flavor...Not only was this good...it nourished both the body and soul. And Hank looked with great favor upon the man whose name was Chef Michel Focqeteau and asked him to go forth and produce great classic French dishes but with the heart and spirit of Creole. And the people came to witness these wondrous acts - and lo! they saw it was good. ■ And it came to pass, I broke bread and witnessed all manners of food. The Crawfish Carolyn, was a dish of fire and brimstone, speaking volumes for Chef Michel. The succulence of the fresh crawfish was in perfect counterpoint to the spicy cream sauce laced with brandy and Parmesan cheese and presented bubbling and piping hot. ■ And so I tarried awhile and beheld a dish of mighty substance, which was prepared before me and verily I say unto you, it too was good. This time, the Baby Veal Christian - a signature of epic proportions, tender slices of pan-sautéed baby veal offered in a rich cream sauce full of flavor with the added ingredients of Port wine and morels. ■ And lo, my eyes were filled with awe at the beauty that this temple of good cooking afforded me. Vaulted beamed ceilings, stained glass windows and the type of seating that would be filled. And as I tarried appreciating the unique ambience, the Chef arrived with a Goliath of a dessert - the classic signature Skip, a veritable mountain of intensely satisfying chocolate, studded with mixed nuts from a myriad lands. And yea again, it too, was good. ■ So my brethren verily I say unto ye, man cannot and will not live by bread alone, when this Christian has so much to offer.

Herbsaint's Cane Braised Beef Shortribs
with Dijon Horseradish Sour Cream
paired with Rémy Martin Extra

HERBSAINT

NEW ORLEANS

Rabbit Fricassee

**paired with
Rémy Martin V.S.O.P**

In the Warehouse District of New Orleans stands Herbsaint, a casual contemporary Bistro-style restaurant. ■ Craig Claiborne, the venerable former New York Times food critic, raconteur and celebrity chef, naturally as a Southerner, insisted *"'N'Owlens'"* was "the home of American Cooking," and not without some foundation. This exciting, intriguing, mysterious city has long held an attraction for the adventurous-dining or otherwise. ■ Blessed with the likes of Paul Prudhomme, Emeril Legasse and Renee Bajeux, the city is now ready to embrace the new development from local talents, James Beard Award recipient for Best Chef in Southwest Region, Susan Spicer and her partner Donald Link at Herbsaint (named after the, esoteric here, but celebrated in France) aperitif Herbsaint. Gourmets have surely heard the continuing buzz about Spice, Inc., a specialty cooking concept and market and Wild Flour Breads. And of course, Bayona, where Spicer has been Executive Chef and co-owner for the last 12 years, and seems particularly at home. But Herbsaint, under the helm of Chef Donald, has since its inception set the town alight with his innovative Modern Amerique Cuisine. ■ Very much a high profile restaurant in this voguish locale of New Orleans, Herbsaint offers adventure and discovery, with items that are at once, flavorful and vibrant. The signature Herbsaint Tomato and

**Shrimp with Green
Chile Grits and
Tasso Cream Sauce**

**paired with
Rémy Martin
V.S.O.P chilled**

Shrimp infused with the aforementioned cordial is a delicious first choice, as is Herb Gnocchi with wild mushrooms, sage and roasted garlic. His eclectic influences are apparent in dishes that range from Beef Short Rib on potato cake with a Dijon mustard horseradish dressing to delicious Rabbit Fricassee served on a bed of homemade pappardelle with wild mushrooms. ■ There is an offbeat whimsy about the cuisine, which is evident in both Link's personality and the ambiance of the restaurant. In the semi-theatre kitchen he wears a baseball cap rather than a toque, and is happiest talking to his regulars and newcomers alike for their take on the meal and their own personal *Herb-sanctification!*

RENE'S
BISTROT

NEW
ORLEANS

Rene Bistrot

■

Chef Rene Bajeux

Right

Grilled Sardines with Octopus Salad

paired with Rémy Martin V.S.O.P iced

"*The meaning of any beautiful created thing is, at least, as much in the soul of him who looks at it, as was in his soul who wrought it*"- *Oscar Wilde* ■ It is a windy wet Big Easy...the storm clouds that were gathering in an angry huddle burst into rain that runs down Bourbon and Burgundy. The rain mutes the sounds of music that usually at this time pulse out a myriad rhythms ...Jazz and Cajun, Blues and Bluegrass.... ■ In this town, as befits its French originations, King Epicure reigns supreme... Paul Prudhomme, Emeril, and of course the "*Big Bear*" himself Rene Bajeux. Very much a folk hero and one of the founding fathers of Contemporary New Orleans cuisine, Bajeux's reputation was secured when, at the Windsor Court Hotel's Grill, his work earned them the much coveted Mobil 5 Star AAA Five-Diamond award. ■ Bajeux's positive approach to a French-based

Southern tradition punctuated with his international variations, interprets well on the menus we are handed. And we are not spoiled for choice with these Bajeux Bijoux. We have traveled for the last eight hours...we are ravenous... we attack with much gusto, our choices of the Galette de Saumon Fume, perfectly crisp potato galettes with a hickory-flavored smoked salmon with a topping of chives and crème fraiche...

■ So far - so good. The ensuing entrees are generous and equally sating. I continue indulgently with my quest for subliminal foie gras and I am not disappointed with Chef Rene's - sautéed with balsamic glazed peaches in a delicate phyllo nest-formidable! And then a touch of guilt (I need to resist any more of this hi-calorie seduction) as I follow with Sebaste - Red fish with clams, orso pasta and shiitake ginger bouillon.

Below

Sauteed Sweetbreads with Morel Cream and Brie Mashed Potatoes

paired with Rémy Martin 1738 Accord Royal

Left

Sebaste

paired with Rémy Martin V.S.O.P iced

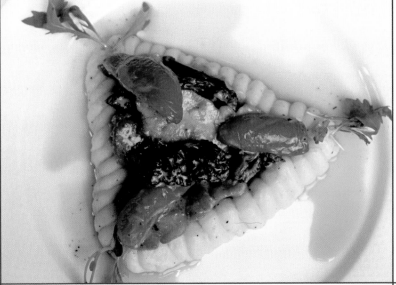

■ Desserts by Joy Jessup are part of the reason why it is such pleasure to eat in this establishment. My winner by far...the Valrhona Chocolate Terrine consisting of a triangle of white chocolate mousse encrusted with a duo of dark and milk chocolate mousse and served with a chocolate sorbet and intensely rich chocolate sauce. ■
Get sated...self-indulge...it's the... Big Easy, Chers!

...TASTE
THE
APPLE...

FELIDIA

NEW YORK

Felidia ■ Chef/Author Lidia Bastianich & Chef Fortunato Nicotra

Blue-Fin Tuna grilled on one side with Toy Box Tomatoes paired with Rémy Martin 1738 Accord Royal iced

I first encountered the impressive credentials of Felidia back in the 80's. East 58th street was then affectionately referred to as *"Restaurant Row"* and in this street of great Italian establishments, Felidia ruled supreme. Felix worked the front and Lidia providing genius in the kitchen, and oh how New York adored them. "Celebrity" then only applied to people like Christopher Walken, David Letterman, Jackie O, Doug Flutie, Yoko, or Woody Allen. And only Graham Kerr galloped around on an embryonic food show. ■ So this is 2003, and what have we done? Another era over and a new one just begun! Truly a Celebrity Chef, with her two widely viewed series *"Lidia's Italian American Kitchen"* and *"Lidia's Italian Table"*, Lidia Mattichio Bastianich still continues to sparkle like the star she is. These days, she is the creator of a totally innovative style of Cucina Italiana, and Master Chef Fortunato Nicotra provides the firepower in the kitchen. The result is a menu of style, elegance and

inimitable flavors. ■ At Felidia, the education of the palate begins with some tempting overtures including a stellar Braised Leek and Corn Ravioli with dry sea scallops and sweet corn kernels - the generously portioned scallops perfectly seared and quite memorably juicy. ■ Two standout entrees that really encapsulate the Felidia philosophy are Blue Fin Tuna grilled ingeniously on one side and served with toy box tomatoes, basil scallions and balsamic vinaigrette; and a classic signature presentation of the Pan-Seared Squab Breast on Chanterelle mushroom farrotto with shredded slow-braised squab legs. ■ And naturally, how can you leave without the final and literal icing on the proverbial cake. The *"Felidian"* desserts are exquisite. Of distinction are the Pistachio Cream Cheese Crostata with raspberry jam, fresh raspberries and pistachio sauce, and a truly indulgent Bittersweet Chocolate Sabayon Cake with Amerene cherries and chocolate sauce. ■ *Consider your palate sated and indeed, educated!*

Pistachio Cream
Cheese Crostata
with Raspberry Jam

paired with
Rémy Martin V.S.O.P

Pan-Seared Squab
Breast on Chanterelle
Mushroom "farrotto"

paired with
Rémy Martin V.S.O.P

Braised Leek and
Corn Ravioli with
Dry Sea Scallops

paired with
Rémy Martin
V.S.O.P chilled

La Caravelle ■ **Chef Troy Dupuy**

"Pleasure is the only thing that one should live for."-Oscar Wilde ■ Forty Years on without missing a beat, Andre and Rita Jammet are widely regarded as part of the founding family of the New York dining scene. Uncompromisingly French in culture and style, their Caravelle reflects some of the haunts for those in search of haute cuisine around the Champs Elysée. ■ Elegant murals depicting the fine de siecle of Paris abound - each splash of color reflected in the sleek mirrors that form an intrinsic part of the stylish interior. ■ The favorite of many prominent New York celebrities including the late Jackie O and JFK Jr., the Media and Manhattan's elite and chic, La Caravelle is an institution. ■ So much for setting the tone... the real fun and enjoyment starts from the moment exquisite, amuses bouche from Chef Troy Dupuy, touch your lips. ■ Dupuy is very serious about food and this is reflected in the precision of his presentation and the

Top Left First Column
Andre & Rita Jammet

Bottom Left First Column
Chef Troy Dupuy

clarity of his perception of taste. But he is equally adept at surprise... Squid Roll with anise hyssop and bean medley...Marinated Tuna and Graylag with seaweed salad and mango vinaigrette...and exemplary Terrine de Foie Gras with a sauternes gelee...impeccable architecture and balance. ■ The quite extensive prix – fixe menu reveals further examples of Dupuy's range...a faithful rendition of Pan Roasted Lobster with Quinoa...Calf's Liver Sweetbreads and Tongue with red mustard leaves

...these are two that really catch the eye and there is more... ■ And, of course, in true French disregard for calories are the desserts! Ones guaranteed to leave you spellbound on this magic Caravelle are a classic Soufflé au Grand Marnier (20 minutes to prepare please) and an inimitable Parfait aux Noix de Macadame, Sorbet au Gingembre... ■ *Well – here's to another Forty, Rita and André!*

Calf's Liver, Sweetbreads and and Onion Confit paired with Charles Heidsieck, Ora

Toasted Macadamia Parfait with Pineapple-Ginger Sherbert

paired with Rémy Martin XO Excellence iced

**Pan Roasted Lobster with
Quinoa, Watercress**

**paired with
Rémy Martin
1738 Accord Royal**

...gue with Red Mustard Leaves
...my Martin V.S.O.P, Cointreau,
Bitters & Orange Slice

**Foie Gras Terrine with
Sauternes Gelee and
Marinated Turnips**

**paired with
Rémy Martin Extra iced**

An icon for over 30 years, this tiny French restaurant in a quiet residential neighborhood was a Gulliver as far as New York's grand cuisine was concerned. I can remember when I first arrived in America, how much the inspirational originator Andre Soltner was lauded by a very critical New York Times Mimi Sheraton. The names then were Soltner, Guerard, Rachou, Margetti and Kovi, But Lutéce was the name on the every cognoscente's lips. ■ Today only the magical Rachou still weaves his wand over at Cote Basque, and the nearest you'll get to Soltner is to hear him making his way down from his flat over the restaurant. ■ The dashing, ex-French Marine David Feau is at the helm these days and can he cook! He has respectfully observed the Soltnerian basics and kept his cooking simple yet classic with imaginative use of delicate spices from foreign shores. An amuse bouche of lemongrass soup signaled an evening of Feau's creativity and his right to continue the Lutécian legend. ■ Sitting in the long angular understated yet classically decorated dining room in the most comfortable of corner banquettes, I enthusiastically embarked on a small degustation of Feau signatures. ■ The Chanterelle Fricassee with apricots and baby spinach and hazelnut, immediately captured the eyes and the palate with its myriad shapes and flavors. This was followed by another Feau staple of his inimitable Black and White Scallops, jumbo scallops perfectly

Lutéce ■ Chef David Fe

"Rock Glass" Warm Chocolate Cake Whipped Cream, Verbena Infusion paired with Rémy Martin Extra

Stuffed and Roasted Quail with Mushrooms and Foie Gras, Artichoke Puree, Spring Onion Jus

paired with Rémy Martin V.S.O.P

Chanterelle and Apricot Fricassee", Baby Spinach and Hazelnut Salad

paired with Rémy Martin 1738 Accord Royal iced

seared and then contrastingly sauced in black and white... The meat entrée signature really was outstanding ...Roasted Quail stuffed with herbs and served with juicy mushrooms and a wonderful seared foie gras, artichoke puree and spring onion jus. Auguste Escoffier did not realize just how many chefs he would inspire by the majestic presentation of his desserts, and although with not quite the same gusto that Escoffier exuded by wheeling in the dessert cart however, Feau makes a more subtle statement by the sheer variety of his afters - especially his beloved favorite (this writer's too!), the "Rock Glass" Warm Chocolate Cake... an indulgent fantasy of still chocolate running deep! Served with freshly whipped cream and verbena infusion...ummm! ■ ...Yes, still up there after all these years!

Black and White Scallops

paired with Rémy Martin V.S.O.P

"Cambia Metro ■ *Dei pazzi e l'amor tetro* ■ *Che lacrime distilla* ■ *Se non ride e sfavilla* ■ *Lamore e fiacco e roco"* –*"Marcello"- La Boheme-Puccini* ■ It is practically impossible to improve perfection, as opera aficionados will testify, but Tony May, with his supremely gifted Chef Odette Fada, almost effortlessly surpasses his highest standards on an annual basis. ■ "3 stars" New York Times, "4 Diamond Award" from AAA, likewise from Mobil, Wine Spectator, Forbes, Esquire, Conde Nast Traveler.... The list is endless. ■ The beautiful décor is quintessential Italian flair abounding with hand-rubbed marmarino walls, terra-cotta tiles, and marble floors. San Domenico is one of the great institutions of New York. ■ And then there is Odette.... Under the inspirational tutelage of Mauro Vincenti, she took Rex 1 Ristorante, in Los Angeles to unprecedented

Opposite Page

Top Right
Tuna Wrapped in Smoked Pork Jowl, Rice Beans & Balsamic Vinegar

paired with Rémy Martin V.S.O.P

Bottom Right
Orange Semifreddo with Amaretto Crust

paired with Rémy Martin 1738 Accord Royal

SAN DOMENICO NEW YORK

Opposite Page

Top Left
Tuna Roe, Orange, Onion, & Sicilian Tomatoes

paired with Rémy Martin V.S.O.P chilled

San Domenico ■ Chef Odette Fada, Tony May & daughter, Marisa

Bottom Left
Veal fillet, Mushroom Broth, Fresh Fava Beans & Potato Croquette

paired with Rémy Martin Extra

heights. Her reputation made, she then joined Tony May at San Domenico, where each day she passionately displays a prodigious talent. Her gift for her signature Italian Classics has the pundits running out of superlatives! ■ Witness her Antipasti: - Air-dried Tuna Roe with orange onion and Sicilian tomatoes, which is the perfect opening gambit at this Roman extravaganza. ■ The cream of the seafood items is the Tuna wrapped in lightly smoked pork jowl, rice beans and balsamic vinegar. I love game, thus it had to be Saddle of Roasted Rabbit with carrots and haricot-vert and a pecorino and garlic sauce - a perfectly, delightful balance of textures and flavors. Another entrée that simply should not be passed over is a classic rendition of Veal Fillet with a light mushroom broth ,fresh fava beans and potato croquette. ■ The dolci here, truly, is a sweet way of life, with an exceptional *"Tira Misu - San Domenico"* - the House Specialty, and of equal status was an Orange Semifreddo with an amaretto crust... your choice is infinite!

...people,

power,

politics,

pabulum...

IN THIS TEMPLE
AS IN THE HEARTS OF THE PEOPLE
FOR WHOM HE SAVED THE UNION
THE MEMORY OF ABRAHAM LINCOLN
IS ENSHRINED FOREVER

WASHINGTON D.C.

"I love food...It may be ok for some chefs to close shop, but not for me... I go home to my family and then I go to sleep dreaming incessantly of how to be nouvelle ...different... to create excitement. I think all things food... Food is simple, with tastes and texture, other world cuisine is fine, but I prefer to avoid over-complication and culinary architecture..." ■ Incomplete without his irrepressible mischievous personality, many of the great guides take great pride and pleasure in listing this icon of icons in the USA. The epitome of the classic

Citronelle ■
Chef Michel Richard

French chef, Richard cuts a majestic swathe as he regally creates behind the theatre kitchen in this *"temple"* - Citronelle. ■ Richard, if he were conjuring up his sorcery in France, would be a constant 3 stars in Guide Michelin. He is hopelessly in love with food and he wears this great passion on his sleeve, whether cooking, eating or just chatting around his huge oak table in the kitchen, the perfect site, to appreciate not only immaculate French cooking, but also to understand much of the great man's

philosophy. ■ Richard is a Piscean and a dreamer and his way with spices and flavor symbolizes the richness and imagination of his fertile mind. One plate in particular that is pure Richard is the Carpaccio Mosaic of Yellowtail, Jambon, Eel, Chicken and Vegetables - aptly described as *"flavors and textures from the earth and ocean"*. The Neptunian coloring of the Asparagus Puree-Encrusted Salmon and its fresh textures added extraordinary dimension to a classic dish, and the delivery of the Lamb entrée was world class in both taste and presentation with the melt

in the mouth delicate Roasted Colorado lamb Medallions, pivotal in our enjoyment. The added innovation of the Cauliflower Couscous served in a miniature sauce pan definitely amused our bouches. ■ And finally a personal favorite of Chef Michel, the Jolie Pomme - a delicate apple sorbet topped with Chantilly and decorated with feather light wafers of green candied apple-taste, delicacy, inspiration, simplicity, and excitement- pure magic from the master!

Salmon, Asparagus Crust, Fresh Morel Sauce paired with Rémy Martin Extra

**Jolie Pomme with Apple Caramel Sauce
paired with Rémy Martin 1738 Accord Royal chilled**

Roasted Colorado
Lamb Loin, Cauliflower
Couscous, Baby
Vegetables, Black
Bean au jus

paired with
Rémy Martin
1738 Accord Royal

Carpaccio Mosaic,
flavor & texture
from Earth & Ocean

paired with
Rémy Martin
V.S.O.P chilled

ETRUSCO TRATTORIA

WASHINGTON D.C.

Opposite Page

Top Left
Assorted Tuscan Crostini

paired with Rémy Martin V.S.O.P

Bottom Left
Grilled Striped White Bass Filet:
Versigliese-style

paired with Rémy Martin V.S.O.P chilled

Bottom Right
Poached White Peach with
Vanilla Ice Cream

paired with Rémy Martin
XO Excellence

" We were the first house to get TV and, when the big game was on, all the village folk gathered around the kitchen table to enjoy the soccer, drink wine and enjoy great Cucina ... We also had the only big wood burning fire...my grandfather, the town consigliore, gave each one, when they left, some wood for them to keep warm as there were no heaters then... ah life was so simple and so unspoilt in those days!"... ■ In the Tuscan hills, sits the centuries-old village of Cercina, Francesco Ricchi's grandfather opened a small grocery store and trattoria. Many years later, young *"Cesco,"* with his parents, turned this into a major success. Continuing this tradition, Chef Ricchi opened Cesco Trattoria, and Etrusco Trattoria in the nation's capital city. ■ Highly regarded by many, for his culinary skills, as well as his humanitarian efforts, Chef Francesco (Cesco to his friends) Ricchi brings family traditions to DC, with Etrusco in the heart of the capital. The split-level interior is brilliantly aspected...the atrium as a focal point, where soaring arched ceilings, decorated with stone washed shades, add depth and style to this fashionable trattoria. So reminiscent of the voguish style of midtown Florence, Etrusco embraces the cognoscenti of classico cucina Italiana with the assurance that dining here will be a night to remember. ■ An absolute must are the multi-flavored Assorted Tuscan Crostini, typical Tuscan food, flavor...and ingredients...all honest and straightforward, but with magnificent variety. For entrees, two fish dishes best reminded us of true Italian home-cooking - Rockfish Livornese adding both drama and flavor with its pungent tomato sauce and ceci... Striped White Bass Versigliese - style (lightly marinated and then slowly grilled). And as for Carni, the Grilled Lamb Tenderloin served with a light lentil salad, was so reminiscent of my first trip to Florence. ■ With restaurants, television appearances on the Discovery Channel's *"Great Chefs of the East,"* and numerous awards, Ricchi has clearly grasped the right blend of good food, ambiance and romance that is sure to spark a love affair with the flavor of a Tuscany, captured so intrinsically, in his cuisine.

Chef "Cesco" Ricchi

Chef Gerard Pangaud

Roasted Breast of Duck
with Plums, Shepherd's Pie
of the Leg "Confites"

paired with Rémy Martin XO Excellence

"2 Stars ... worth a detour ... 3 stars – worth the journey" – Guide Michelin ■ Chef/Owner Gerard Pangaud is a master chef who was awarded two Michelin stars at the age of 27 making him the youngest chef ever to receive such an honor and is currently the only two-starred chef working in the United States. ■ Located in the oasis-like Macpherson Square, in the heart of the nation's capital is this stylish pavement bistro. Uncompromisingly French, with eclectic artifacts and objets d'art (very much a reflection of Chef Proprietor Gerard Pangaud's taste and Puckishness) Gerard's Place is truly one of this city's culinary treasures. Set back from a charming front terrace, this restaurant showcases a menu of studied elegance and skillful understatement. Pangaud is an inspirational cook. He adapts modern technique with the freshest of ingredients and the resulting dishes are at once both artistic and flavorful.
■   *"Every meat presented its own natural aroma...every vegetable its own shade of verdure"*-Lady Morgan describing French Grand Chef Carene's brilliant cooking at a Baron De Rothschild dinner during the 19th century. ■   His seasonal menu is the proverbial treat, with such teasing appetizers as the Cold Vichyssoise of Sweet Potato perfumed with ginger and anis and an altogether surprising presentation of Sautéed Scallops with sweet garlic flan and parsley mousse, transporting you to the bustle of the Champs Elysees. And then with a sleight of hand, he switches your culinary odyssey to Provencal with a classic Gigot Confit with ratatouille and pesto with an heirloom tomato salad...More magic and you are appreciating the aromas and taste of Burgundy with a Roasted Breast of Duck with "Parmentier" of duck confit and braised local peaches. ■ And, of course, for those of you where *"custom cannot stale"* your sweet tooth, try the quite exotic Exotic Fruit Soufflé with roasted pineapple and a caramel of spices. ■ Still not sated! Then M. Pangaud will entertain you and indulge your culinary ambitions with his series of cooking classes at the restaurant on selected Saturdays... *"Well worth the journey"*!

GERARD'S PLACE

WASHINGTON D.C.

Bottom Right
**Scallops with Parsley
Mousse**

**paired with
Rémy Martin
1738 Accord Royal**

Left
Exotic Fruit Souffle

**paired with
Rémy Martin
1738 Accord Royal**

MELROSE

WASHINGTON D.C.

Somerset Maugham once observed "To eat well in England, you should have breakfast three times a day!" ■ Thank Heaven that Melrose is not in England and that you only have to indulge yourself once there, tasting the eclectic inspired menu of Washington favorite, Brian McBride, to eat well. ■ McBride is the consummate Chef's chef. He has earned a quite enviable reputation and is probably one of the most respected hotel chefs in the business today. Melrose has been his charge for over a decade and it has always remained one of D.C.'s most lauded restaurants. ■ Providing the tranquility that is sorely needed in this city of hustle and bustle, power games and high stake political machinations, Melrose is a veritable oasis for the hungry and fatigued. A blissful cascading fountain provides the perfect canvas for a quiet yet exciting al fresco meal on the spacious terrace. If you prefer more sophisticated surroundings, then a table by the window in the split-level, quite handsome dining room is a very rewarding option. ■ McBride's menu is quite a surprise. Drawing from rich experience, he brings together Contemporary American fare, which offers quite meaningful eclectic pairings of flavors, shapes and textures. He is also quick to realize the value of light cuisine. His starter of the Pan-seared Maine Divers Scallops, flash seared, with white asparagus and black truffle vinaigrette, is decidedly exquisite, tasteful and hits the spot. As entrées, our choices of Roulade of Yellow Tail (resembling a large tuna roll) Scallop and Green Oonion with baby corn, water chestnuts, chinese broccoli and cilantro vinaigrette, and the Loin of Rabbit encased in Slow-cooked Leg with apricot and sage over mixed baby carrots and presented in a Madeira Sauce, illustrated quite dramatically McBride's sharp eye for detail, a penchant for Far Eastern influences and a palate for definitive taste - for me it was *"Lead on McBride"* (Sorry Bill!). ■ And then it was time for maximum indulgence and again McBride's discerning stewardship in the kitchen pays dividends for the restaurant's reputation and the customer's appreciation. An ingenious presentation of Strawberry and Passion-fruit Soups with buttermilk panacotta and macadamia nut brittle, left me in no doubt that as hotel restaurants go, Melrose is the place to visit, sample and enjoy.

Chef Brian McBride

Opposite Page

Top Left
**Loin of Rabbit encased
in Slow Cooked Leg**

**paired with Rémy Martin
1738 Accord Royal**

Bottom Left
Strawberry & Passion Fruit Soup

**paired with Rémy Martin
1738 Accord Royal**

Top Right
**Pan Seared Maine
Diver Scallops**

**paired with
Rémy Martin V.S.O.P**

Bottom Right
Roulade of Yellow Tail

**paired with
Rémy Martin V.S.O.P**

THINGS TA
IN SMALL

TE BETTER
HOUSES.

VICTORIA,
QUEEN OF
ENGLAND

General Manager
Adi Modi

Executive Chef
Vikram Sunderam

Lamb Nehari

paired with
Rémy Martin
XO Excellence

The UK 's Number One, the B
as the Kama Sutra to Indian
with the accolades - This spe
conservatory and limpid pon
Kidman, Cruise, Hanks, Hawn
who simply crave for a great
much charm, by London's er
Club fame), Adi Modi, "B.B.'
dining scene. Undergoing rec
elegant murals depicting sce
including the historic Red Fo
tastes, are so inimitably India.
words of the irrepressible Mic
Always the best way to star
Chaas, a liquid yoghurt, whic
Mumbai style (salted with ging
and dried mustard seeds.) Cert

preparation for the ensuing f
Vikram Sunderam, is the othe
experience and judgment, an
fare has for many years, dazzle
The starters, the essence of va
(crispy fried baby spinach with
covered with sweet yoghurt an
Dum ka Bater (Fresh quail, b
cashew nut puree a special
Dharbar continues with the de
from Lucknow, of Lamb Shan
gravy) or if you like vegetar
especially the Bhindi Jaipuri -
and onions, tossed with chilli,
sensual profusion of flavors co
find out for yourselves and disc
life!

BOMBAY
BRASSERIE

LONDON

y Brasserie is to Indian cuisine
ophy. Since opening, replete
ar restaurant, with imposing
tinues to delight the likes of
rosnan, not to mention those
an"! ■ Presided over, with
herman Billingsley (of Stork
uly an icon to London's chic
d subtle refurbishment, with
from the late 18th century,
Delhi… the sights, scents and
experience here will be in the
Winner, "truly historic"! ■
e is with a delicate fragrant
be ordered sweet, salted, or
esh coriander, a hint of cumin
this refreshing drink is perfect

Palak Pakodi Chaat

**paired with
Rémy Martin
V.S.O.P iced**

Himalayan Peaks

**paired with
Rémy Martin
V.S.O.P chilled**

n of spices and flavors. Chef
son for the BB's success. His
s passion for regional Indian
e palates of the faithful. ■
y, include Palak Pakodi Chaat
ions tomatoes and black salt
marind chutney-delish!) or the
d with yoghurt almond and
am masala) Your Epicurean
te Lamb Nehari (a signature,
rved with a fine flavorsome
dishes these are exceptional
B. special of crispy fried okra
mango and cumin. ■ This
ls me to urge you - go taste -
r what to many is truly way of

Hidden in the heart of Mayfair, underneath a cobbled archway is this stylish courtyard restaurant. Just a stone's throw away from the pomp and circumstance (and haute cuisine!) of famed Claridges; this unconventional hot venue is London's best-kept secret. ■ The partnership of Jamie Barber, Geoffrey Moore and the gifted Chef David Rood has elevated this celeb haunt into a bar and grill of note. Hush is sophisticated, fun and literally buzzes with the beautiful people, even a Bond girl- type or two. There is a setting to indulge every mood… bustling casual brasserie…the al fresco romance of the courtyard, where lovers meet across a Kir or two…the sleek gray tones and splashes of lilac and lavender…complete with the private, sunken- floored Boudoir…an elegant dining room and bar that would befit a suave discerning James Bond. I am sure Mr. Moore Snr. had a hand in this, especially as the well –balanced wine list reveals the classic Bollinger Special Cuvee and Dom Perignon '95. Indeed, the cellar- full of distinguished varieties including a delectable

Chef David Rood

…nearby Bond Street …Secret Service… 007… Spy …Hush - Get It?

Corton –Charlemagne Grand Cru and a Gevrey Chambertin Premier Cru- certainly emphasizes the licence to thrill!. ■ And then of course, exceptional modern cuisine from the precocious talents of a prodigious Rood… Pick of his starters, include the Baby Asparagus and Watercress Salad, with truffle crème fraiche, and the Rare Breast of Duck with mache and crispy pancetta salad, which was preceded by a melt -in –your- mouth, amuse bouche of Foie Gras and Caramelized Apple terrine!. ■ This view to a fill continues with a classic rendition of Grilled Halibut with crispy red onion and pecorino pithivier, baby leek, and sauce lie de vin, and Roast Breast of Poussin, wrapped in prosciutto with aubergine caviar - *can the Lad really cook!* ■ The arrival of a traditional Crème Brulee and a really Sticky Toffee Pudding with crème fraiche - both exceptional signatures- served with copious measures of Remy VSOP, herald a satisfying but reluctant close this *"double- oohh!" extravaganza."*

Millefeuille of King Scallops with sweet peas and artichokes with sauce beaumes de venise

paired with Rémy Martin V.S.O.P iced

HUSH

LONDON

Roast Noissette of Lamb with Truffle braised cabbage Sautéed girolles and lemon thyme jus

paired with Rémy Martin V.S.O.P

Pink Champagne Jelly

paired with Rémy Martin V.S.O.P chilled

Le Gavroche is truly a national institution, indeed as the sleeve notes state in Michel Roux's commemorative Le Gavroche Cookbook (Cassell & Co) *"The ethics principles and excellence...have remained unchanged and unchallenged for 31 years ....on of the best of its kind in the world...the creation of Michel and Albert Roux"* ■ The Roux dynasty brilliantly continues as Michel Roux, inspired by his legacy, develops brilliance after brilliance, in a cuisine that although strongly rooted in France, is so superlatively different. There is magic here the minute you walk through the famous doors. The lobby bar both vivacious and colorful with a provocative glow from rich crimson hues catches your eye. ■ Gavroche is provocative, seductive and challenging. Roux himself, is a charmer with the same humor and twinkle as his revered "*papa*" Albert. Rather, like his idol Eric Cantona the legendary Manchester United soccer player who transformed that Club into world-beaters once again, he's bold... he's controversial... making his product too, world class. ■ It has been a long time...a matter of perhaps 20 years... I am curious... Is the son really as good as they say he is... can he repeat a tremendous history? The answers come faster than a young Georgie Best in his halcyon days... I am privileged to visit a kitchen of an abundance of spirit, soul, humor and familiar togetherness... from the young future gavroches, watching with great intensity, the master's deftness with knife and fingers making his beautiful craft so easy. ■ At the front, the revered Silvano is at work... table- hopping, greeting, accommodating, pampering, flirting with a fast filling room. ■ Then it's show-time... Like a magician's hat...surprise, punctuated by more surprise... each act seemingly impossible to follow, but the supreme sorcerer weaves his magic besting each previous offering. ■ Perfect spicing and variation, no doubt due to his extensive travels in the

"The ethics principles and excellence...have remained unchanged & unchallenged for 31 years ....on of the best of its kind in the world...the creation of Michel and Albert Roux"

Duck Pastilla with Foie Gras

paired with Rémy Martin V.S.O.P iced

old country with the masters as well the Far East. Overwhelming evidence is a menu that always delivers. Fresh Crab Meat Salad with lime and peanut oil pepper and tomato mousse, a Coquilles St Jacques with a five-spice sauce are two starters that simply set the standard and the tone of this massive talent. ■ Then a twinkling surprise dish is placed before me by Silvano - a Hot Foie Gras and Crispy Pancake of Duck dusted and flavoured with cinnamon, followed by a spectacular Roast Pigeon from Bresse with spiced red wine pears and crispy pancake... ■ Still Roux doesn't miss a trick, as with a flourish his Poached Spiced Pear with pink pralines arrives ...the presentation first class... the taste infinite. ■ Leaving this effervescent dining room absolutely sated, I have only one nagging question remaining for this prodigious talent "... *Why Manchester United and not Arsenal, Michel?!*"

LE GAVROCHE

LONDON

Spicy Fresh Crab Salad

**paired with
Rémy Martin
Extra iced**

Poached Pear with Pink Pralines
paired with Rémy Martin V.S.O.P chilled

Ebullient as ever, Richard Shepherd, CBE is still doing it his way and naturally, we have to cheer him on. He is the man who created the *"celebrity"* in *"Chef"*! Who else could satisfy the faithful with such offerings as *"bangers 'n' mash"* and *"cod and chips"?!* ■ Langan's and Shepherd have become an institution. Now over 25 years old, this remarkable restaurant is a "must- visit" when in London. And it's not just the food that has pleased so many for so long. It is truly one of the great "ambience" establishments in the world. Recessions-phooey! World crises- forget them! Langan's is a symbol of freedom for its worldwide clientele. The perfect place in which to just escape reality's harshness, get intoxicated and fall in love with London, everybody and everything! ■ Shepherd, originally, determined, with genius Peter Langan (sadly deceased), to offer the public freedom where you could order anything from a pudding to a full blown out meal. Dress up or down (Peter was frequently dressed down!) You could even go "au naturel" as one socialite did! But they wanted fun and to "cock a snook" at the establishment! ■ Today, it is very much the venue for celebrity and people -watchers and still extremely reasonably priced. And the Michelin -starred Shepherd, as ever, is resolute in his approach to top notch, yet simple honest cooking. ■ For me no visit to my home-town is complete without a dinner or two at Langan's. In fact, even my idiot son (actually

LANGAN'S BRASSERIE

LONDON

Richard Shepherd & Langan's team

beloved) and his mates look forward to those visits. Nothing gives them or me greater pleasure than to enjoy the company, Shepherd's menu, puffing on our cigars like men of the world, whilst drinking in an atmosphere, particularly on the weekend, that is so priceless. ■ A recent meal there was memorable...Spinach Soufflé with Anchovy sauce that immediately made my top twenty dishes worldwide. Perfect texture and shape- and an immediate hit with my young companions. This was followed by the Fresh Salmon Fishcake in a parsley sauce-needless to say we were practically licking our` plates- so good was it! Then more down to earth Shepherd-ism, with an immaculate Roast Best End of Lamb with Provencal Herbs. ■ It was a toss up between Crème Brulee (a classic!), Banana and Toffee Cheesecake (marvelously gooey!) and of course the ubiquitous Treacle Tart...controversy raged...insanity prevailed...all three arrived... and the gastronomic orgy sadly, but spectacularly, came to an end! ■ As for that ambience- show me a place where, as you enter, the sheer electricity cheerfully assaults your composure. The décor has over the years, had a few retouches here and there, but in the main, you can still enjoy its audacious bubbling fin de siecle style and one of the largest collections of original art by seventies wunderkind David Hockney. ■ Nice one - Richard!

**Langan's
Brasserie**

**Spinach Soufflé &
Anchovy Sauce**

**paired with
Rémy Martin
V.S.O.P**

**Salmon Fishcake &
Parsley Sauce**

**paired with
Rémy Martin
XO Excellence**

Roast Best End of Lamb with Provencal Herbs

paired with Rémy Martin XO Excellence

Creme Brulée

paired with Rémy Martin V.S.O.P iced

"*The table remains a powerful symbol of friendship and a celebration of Life...My food doesn't punish you, it's modern . . . building up a balance . . . I've redefined the food . . . this is my vision.*" ■ Welcome to the philosophy of one of the world's greatest chefs- Master Chef Patron Raymond Blanc and to his inspirational dining hostelry-Le Manoir aux Quat' Saisons- the Pride of the Relais and Chateaux Association and a feather in the cap for Orient Express Hotels, its new partner. ■ Raymond Blanc, these days is clearly in love and as they say all the world loves a lover- no surprise therefore to find that glorious late summer day a garden packed with Blanc fans perusing menus, savoring the descriptions in a menu that constantly exceeds excellence. ■ A melodious tolling of the nearby church's bell peals out at noon... the Midwich cuckoo calls... its gentle echoing across the beautifully tranquil countryside (just 45 miles from London)... Gently sipping flutes of superbly mixed Kir Royale... browsing through an amazing menu... prepared by his outstanding protégé...and Choice... the soul of Blanc's philosophy...the Menu Gourmand, the perfect opportunity to sample Chef Blanc's seasonal specialties, or a la Carte, for his celebrated signatures. ■ The bright conservatory reveals a welcoming

Café Créme Chocolate Cup and Saucer paired with Rémy Martin Extra iced

"...the topic of sex... ...for the dessert..."

LE MANOIR AUX QUAT' SAISONS

LONDON

ambience and several happy diners, all sharing Blanc's dream. This is all about reputation... legendary polished service... remarkable Michelin stars French cuisine... wines from an impeccable cellar... And always this perfect harmony with his food... The appetizers are a revelation, particularly Foie Gras Terrine with soused cherries, mango chutney, and Spiced Duck (sublime!) and a Ravioli of Cornish Lobster and Sea Scallop in a lemon verbena bouillon. ■

Bringing balance to an inspired meal are; a Braised Cornish Fillet of Turbot and Scallops with garden vegetables, wild mushrooms and chive scented jus: and, in keeping with Blanc's traditional French upbringing, Pan Fried Veal kidneys, Burgundy Snails and a puree of shallots, red wine jus with green Chartreuse. ■ And finally - *"...the topic of sex for the dessert... at which point my extremely devoted Catholic mother would hurriedly leave the room..."*- the desserts, from Patissier- extraordinaire, Benoit Blin... include unquestionably, one of the most spectacular and creative I've yet to see - the Coffee Cup - a deep intense chocolate demi- tasse filled with crème and topped with a scoop of vanilla bean ice cream. . . Maitre-Chef Raymond is indeed in love and I swear you can sense the muses at work... *Bravo... Bravo... Bravo!*

Foie Gras Terrine,
Soused Cherries,
Mango Chutney
& Spiced Duck

paired with
Rémy Martin
V.S.O.P iced

Raymond Blanc

Pan Fried Venison
Medallion, "Grand
Veneur" sauce spiked
with bitter Cocoa,
braised Chestnuts

paired with
Rémy Martin
XO Excellence

Roasted Baby Turbot on
a bed of dried scented
herbs, Red Wine Jus &
Rosemary Butter

paired with
Rémy Martin
V.S.O.P

Page 210

MOSIMANN'S LONDON

Fillet of Lamb with a mustard and herb crust

paired with Rémy Martin XO Excellence

...all sweetness and light...

Marinated Salmon with Cornish Crabmeat

paired with Rémy Martin V.S.O.P iced

Anton Mosimann is a legend ... recognition from Michelin ...a plethora of awards including the rare Croix du Chevalier du Merite Agricole...celebrity chef appearances in broadcasting... Food has always been a religion. The Dorchester, where at 28 he made such a memorable debut, was, during his reign, considered by the more discerning, the temple of contemporary haute cuisine... Now, having redefined *"taste"* in British cooking, the master chef has selected a former Presbyterian church to be an ideal shrine for preaching culinary Excellence. ■ The interior is, all sweetness and light... ingeniously designed...paneling and the lofty beamed ceiling... a majestic glass chandelier... a quaintly appointed gallery bar and lounge replete with mischievous cartoons and amusing memorabilia revealing, surprisingly, an impish sense of humour... lingering over an excellently prepared martini observing below famous faces indulging in wondrous fare...More hallmarks of Mosimann-esque humor... lazy frogs... the odd crab... duck and chicken... nestling amidst the sparkling red black and yellow edged Mosimann plates set on sparkling tablecloths... ■ Unquestionably, there is luxury in these surroundings...an ambience of unhurried pampering, ...as an indulgent master sommelier guides you through a flawless wine list. But the food.... ■ Fine Chicken Liver Parfait with warm pistachio brioche, Warm Oriental Duck with vegetables and especially the Marinated Salmon and Cornish Crab with Spring onions and limes are all an excellent way to open your account. ■ The entrees are fine examples of Mosimann at his trois etoiles best... the very essence of perfection, such as Dover Sole Caprice breaded and served with homemade mango chutney; a Mosimann classic, a

Chef Anton Mosimann

Peppered Pineapple with Crème de Cacao Sauce paired with Rémy Martin V.S.O.P iced

definitive Steak Tartare *"Belfry"*, and an absolute must - the Saddle of Welsh Lamb with a chive crust. ■ Mosimann well knows what Brits like...all things sweet, and of course what could be sweeter than his dessert offerings...My eyes widen at the variety… a Trio of Creme Brulees, Anton's very own Bread and Butter Pudding... the very exotic Roasted Pineapple in a Crème de Cacao sauce topped with homemade vanilla ice cream... all unashamedly sticky comestibles... and all very much appreciated by this Brit! ■ Offering several forms of membership, Mosimann's is a *"member's only"* club and boasts private rooms, which periodically are sponsored by such prestigious companies as Gucci, Davidoff and Mont Blanc for themed occasions. But certainly to Mosimann disciples, it is a hallowed ground where sublime cuisine and outstanding wines always marry in perfect harmony.

**Cushions of Scottish Smoked Salmon filled with
Fresh Salmon and Dill paired with Rémy Martin XO Excellence**

TURNER'S

LONDON

Brian Turner is a house- hold name with his BBC Television series, a consultant chef for a prominent airline, and he is a bit good! But what he really enjoys is the sanctuary of his beloved kitchen, delightfully located in this prestigious square. ■ On entering the restaurant, you can appreciate an oasis of abounding tranquility and style a far cry from the madding crowd of nearby Marble Arch and Oxford Street. ■ Mr. Turner is the consummate perfectionist. Not only one of Britain's most distinguished Master Chefs, but as a gifted teacher, he is also recognized for developing new talent. ■ Disdainfully ignoring fads and culinary whims, and with no-nonsense, (he is a Yorkshire lad after all!) Turner continues consistently to *"get it right"*. ■ Like his legendary namesake, Turner, has a definitive style adding vibrant colors and flavors to his rich culinary canvas. His is a display of such modern uncompromisingly English fare, including an absolutely superb Steak and Kidney Plate Pie with oysters and gravy (I really craved for this one!), Best End of English Lamb, with onion potato cake and basil jus (*"England's Green and Pleasant Land"?*) and a real comfort food item: Stratford upon Avon Best Pork *"Bangers"* with Mash and Onion gravy ■ This eye-catching exhibition of Turner impressions continues with further sweet touches and accents. Not to be passed up, are Blueberry and Fudge Bread and Butter pudding and Steamed Treacle Sponge Pudding with Double Cream Custard- which I haven't more enjoyed since school dinners, when we were fed this to combat the cold from wearing short pants in winter! ■ Or, if you can, for once, ignore the demands of the inner child, then you can be sensible and enjoy the more mature tones of his British Cheeses of the Week - quite perfect with that Port or chilled VSOP. ■ *...Nice one, Lad!*

Top
Raspberry Arctic Roll

**paired with
Rémy Martin
Extra**

Center
Best End of English Lamb, Onion Potato and Basil Jus

**paired with
Rémy Martin
V.S.O.P**

I FEEL A REC
THEME, WHICH
COOK CAN PL
WITH A VARIAT

PE IS ONLY A
AN INTELLIGENT
AY EACH TIME
ON.

MADAME
BENOIT, CHEF
AND WRITER

Terrine of Duck Foie Gras from Vendeen with Spicy Apple Chutney

paired with Rémy Martin Extra chilled

Smoked Bacon-Wrapped Quail with Cabbage and Poultry Stuffing

paired with Rémy Martin Extra

"Prunes & Oranges" with a Heather Honey Syrup

paired with Rémy Martin Extra

**Sommelier Du Monde
Phillipe Faure-Brac &
Chef Jean-Andre Lallican**

It's also no coincidence that Claudel himself came from a farming background where quality food and great wines - both products from the soil - made for a sound marriage. ■ Bistrot du Sommelier is the restaurateurs' restaurant. The spectacularly creative duo, Faure-Brac and Master Chef Jean-Andre Lallican continue to delight in pursuit of the perfect plate with wine. Located in a less fashionable area of Paris, the whole idea of Bistrot du Sommelier is to avoid faddish cuisine. Instead exists a genuine desire to impart philosophy and taste with a view to educate attitudes and opinion of food and wine. Even the surroundings eschew fussiness and faux cutting-edge décor. Rather, one is able to sit in casual surroundings, relaxed and in good company, sampling honest yet innovative food from Chef Lallican whilst enjoying the passionate attention of a true master of wines. ■ As befits the World's Best Sommelier and an author in his own right (he is currently planning a new book on cuisine and classic wines - you must read his Les Grands Vins du Siecle), Faure-Brac commands the art of palate, texture and flavor, and has a partner worthy of the same credentials. The result is a continuing degustation, where an enterprising menu is tailor-made for the patron with appropriate wine pairings. ■ Your expectancy heightens with some appetizing starters, which include Goat-cheese with country ham and purple artichokes, and Szechwan Style Peppered Duckling Breast with grilled mushrooms marinated in sesame oil. Pick of the entrees from Chef Jean-Andre include a variation on a theme - a formidable Seafood Cassolette with onion compote, and a very tender and tasty Domes Quail, roasted with spices and served with an apple crumble. ■ The desserts include a Rice Pudding with caramelized spices and dried fruits, and a Millefeuille of Dark and Milk Chocolate with banana marmalade, green apples and a bitter orange coulis - total indulgence and why not? ■ ...and of course I'll entrust the wine recommendation to the world's leading expert!

"Le Vin est le professeur du gout...liberateur de l'esprit et l'illuminateur de l'intelligence"-Paul Claudel

BISTROT DU SOMMELIER

FRANCE

Chef Yannick Alleno has started the gig of his young life at Le Meurice, having stunned a critical Parisian dining fraternity with his prodigious cooking stint at Le Scribe. Within weeks of his advent at this famed hotel, the pundits are applauding his brilliantly presented plates. ■ And what a dramatic stage for this epicurean debut...Antique mirrors, crystal chandeliers, original mosaic flooring, soaring ceiling with spectacular frescoes, all fit for a king. Inspired by the Salon de la Paix in Versailles, the classic historic elegance of this famous grand salle hearkens back to the days of that great Parisian Colossus and the father of them all – Auguste Escoffier. Will Alleno one day be compared to the *"King"* - *Que sera, sera?* But one thing is assured - his quiet understated passion. ■ And all the time there is a grin as wide as the Seine on his handsome features as he joyfully

Top Left
Crab Claw Meat
flavored with
Citrus Fruit

paired with
Rémy Martin
V.S.O.P iced

Center
Chocolate Cube with
refreshing Mint

paired with
Rémy Martin Extra

"He is a Guide Michelin trois etoile - in-waiting. His name is usually mentioned in the same breath as Ducasse and Robuchon..."...his cuisine defies qualifications and trends...the incarnation of pure pleasure." (Gault Millaud). "...the new generation of talented chefs who successfully combine classic traditions with sensible modern style..." –(Joel Robuchon).

hustles and gently cajoles his rapt staff below stairs...it was with much joyful anticipation that I peruse the Menu Degustation: a mere bagatelle at 150 euros per person. My private heaven begins with the superb delicate textures of the Chicken with Duck Foie Gras in a cauliflower roquefort sauce. The epicurean indulgence continues with Smoked Salmon served with encrusted potatoes and a pear puree topped with caviar. Then a variation on a classic Paella containing all kinds of Neptunian delights... With an effortless switch of gears he presents his celebrated Homard Bleu au Vin de Chateau Chalon served with hazelnut macaroni. For the main dish, for me there is only one choice... the Pigeon Breast ... aah... eat your heart out Talleyrand! ■ ...this was, for me, a rapturous epicurean experience...You lucky, lucky Parisians for having this chef all to yourselves!

LE MEURICE

FRANCE

Chef Yannick Alleno

Below
**Sautéed Veal
Sweetbreads**

**paired with
Rémy Martin
Extra chilled**

Top Right
**Pistachio Shortbread
Balm Flavored
Strawberries and
Crystallized Rhubarb**

paired with
Rémy Martin
V.S.O.P chilled

Chef Christophe David

Left Bottom
**Authentic Grilled
Sirloin French-style
Steak**

paired with
Rémy Martin Extra

LE PARK

FRANCE

Christophe David has arrived... He strides like the young Colossus he is, cutting a huge swathe in style, innovation and personality. Literally taking a skeptical Paris by a storm not seen since Bastille, this charismatic young chef is close to earning one of the fastest Michelin etoiles ever awarded. ■ Chef David, with the Hyatt Group's support, and since the opening of this sparkling new Ed Tuttle-inspired hotel and its restaurant, has won over a very skeptical Paris, with his "l'air vif" approach to contemporary French Cuisine. ■ The result is a menu non-pareil. Artistic, delicate, unique structured with balance and taste, huge oceanic swells of flavour, coupled with a masterful choice of wines... A Bocuse protégé- (what else!) and stints at Taillevent and Lucas Carton with Senderens, virtually guarantee that Le Park is up for a very long run indeed. ■ David's talent is so clear as he powers like the Rugby full back he once was

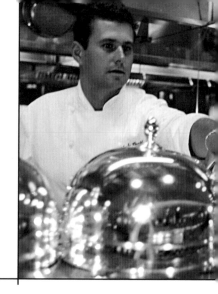

"I can no longer keep silent: to the glory of an art which, since you have exercised it, has become as noble as it was already essential... you are, Monseigneur, one of the best cooks in France..."- The Epitre Dedicatoire of Le Cuisinier Gascon to the Prince de Dombes. (All Manners of Food by Stephen Mennell-Illini Books)

through his day, like a man possessed with indefatigable energy... Arborio Risotto with ceps from Correze with argali and parmigiano reggiano, Landes Duck Foie Gras (grilled on their trademark Charcoal Pit) with autumn fruits with crispy gingerbread honey and cinnamon...a superbly flavored Wagyu – the delicate quintessential black beef from Japan...What makes one's experience so memorable is that this chef is not afraid to break the culinary ceiling with such a joyful and liberated use of a myriad spices. ■ Gastronomy as an expression is so over used... but not here in this elegant stylish cutting edge neo - Classic rotunda replete with the abstracts of celebrated Indian artist Viswanadhan... not at the Park Hyatt-Vendome or Le Park, where a dedication to Cuisine D'art abounds... with its stunningly conceived dining room and avant-garde facades and interiors.

**Roasted Langoustines
in Salted Butter,
Tomato Chutney
with Herbs**

**paired with
Rémy Martin
XO Excellence chilled**

**Wild Lobster from
Roscoff in a Curry with
Browned Apple**

**paired with
Rémy Martin
Extra chilled**

Chef Thierry Verrat

Left
**Langoustines with
Orange Juice & Saffron**

**paired with
Rémy Martin
V.S.O.P iced**

Right
**Roquefort with Pear
and Spicy Chutney**

**paired with
Rémy Martin V.S.O.P**

Far Right
**Tarte au Chocolat
and Macadamia**

**paired with
Rémy Martin
1738 Accord Royal**

I first met Thierry Verrat, ove
Rémy Martin, I was introduced
wife Patricia at their delig
located in the idyllic town of
the placid waters of the Cha
drenched afternoon, I take in a
the locals. Their humour is no
gambit with the passion of a
am sitting on the terrace ...I'a
can hear the kitchen preparir
Despite its rustic location, t
sophistication of La Ribaudier
and his cuisine underline a
prime product – Cognac. Indee
decanters and bottles of war
excellence. ■ All his in
Cognacais harvest and Verrat
promote them in his pursuit o
to present a variety of dishes
as much as sophisticated - Fi
pineau, spinach and pine nu
Crayfish with cognac, Slices of
from Robelines and piquan
paysan...Charente Snails in the
Cheek with country wine a
simplicity itself, Black Puddir
jars... ■ Indeed it is easy to
than simply a Michelin high
Verrat states -"*Buying it to st
making a dream come true*"...
adventure for most of us, beyo

> **"The first skill of a restaurateur is to be the ambassador of the land that he serves..."**

ear ago, when, as a guest of
this remarkable Chef and his
restaurant La Ribaudiere,
rg- Charente on the banks of
e   ■   It is a beautiful sun
me of Boules being played by
t on me as they contest every
ick Viera in a soccer match. I
anquil, l'air vif...behind me I
There is much frivolity...   ■
is a studied elegance and
cor. In many respects, Verrat
icated tribute to the area's
t is hard to ignore the myriad
amber tones of this spirit of
dients are the fruits of the
menu shows his readiness to
re taste.   ■   Thus he is able
t are so uniquely indigenous
of Pike Perch with shallots,
Pike Mousse and Puree of
t Duck Foie Gras with apples
honey caramel...and some,
d fashioned way...Braised Ox
potatoes in goose fat. Or
(Boudin noir) in preserving
e that La Ribaudiere is more
ated restaurant. As Thierry
an adventure was a way of
rtainly dining here is truly an
our wildest dreams!

LA RIBAUDIERE

FRANCE

**Veal Chop with
Figs & Plums**

**paired with
Rémy Martin Extra**

durch 28 Länder der Welt
DECAZEVILLE / VILLE
43 pays à pied,
21 ans

STELLA ARTOIS
CAFE
W-C

ONE OF THE
THINGS ABOU
WAY WE MU
STOP WHATEV
ARE DOING
OUR ATTENTIO